Letters of Recommendation

Letters
of
Recommendation

Maxine McClintock

The Reflective Commons
Collaboratory for Liberal Learning
New York, New York

Letters of Recommendation
By Maxine McClintock

The Reflective Commons
Collaboratory for Liberal Learning
106 Morningside Drive, #62
New York, NY 10027

publications@liberallearning.org
www.liberallearning.org

Library of Congress Control Number: to be added

ISBN: 978-1-937828-01-1 Hardback
ISBN: 978-1-937828-00-4 Paperback
Copyright © 2013 by Maxine McClintock

CONTENTS

Contents v

Foreword vii

To my students and colleagues xv

1. Emilia Starts the School Year with Writer's
   Block and Second Thoughts 1

2. Doc Offers a Not-So-Modest Proposal 6

3. Emilia Regards Teachers as Persons of
   Interest... 10

4. What Are We Talking About When We Talk
   About Education? 14

5. Emilia Rereads Randolph Bourne's Essay and
   Writes One of Her Own 23

6. The Tale of a Queen Bee and a Double Life............ 28

7. Emilia Launches a Campaign to Pop the Bubble
   at Alden 37

8. Doc Lays the Groundwork for a Teachable
   Moment 43

9. Blind-Sided by Good Intentions 49

10. Cultivating the Fine Art of Detachment.................... 53

11. Emilia is Definitely Not in a Holiday Mood 57

12. To Move On, Emilia Is Advised to Let Go................. 62

13. Emilia Stands Her Ground.................................... 69

Independent Study Proposal William James 70

14. Learning to Love the Questions Themselves 72

15. The Year Ends with a Rapprochement and a
    Walk 74

16. Investigating the Octopus that Threatened
    Harvard 80

17. Doc Recommends Thinking Like a Historian........... 85

18. The World Turned Upside Down and Inside Out 87

19. Attending to the "Fall of Icarus" 90

20. Emilia Follows Her Nose 94

21. Doc Gives Citizen Emilia Something to Ponder 101

22. Becoming Acquainted with the Young Man
    from Wisconsin 104

23. Nuts and Bolts 108
Independent Study Schedule Emilia Carlyle 110
24. For Emilia the Issue Is One of Character 111
25. Doc Counsels Emilia to Keep Complexity in
    Mind as She Investigates Character 117
26. Character's Corrupters, or Bigness and the
    Club Opinion 119
27. Doc Draws an Analogy between Working-Out
    and Exercising Reason 123
28. To Know a Good Man When You See One 128
29. Occupying Interstices to Raise Democracy's
    Tone 134
30. On the Outs with the Cancún Contingent 138
31. Doc Makes the Case for Solitude 141
32. Conversation about a Community Activist and
    Other Dinner Party Illuminations 144
33. Emilia Voices Reservations about Utopian
    Visions 147
34. 'Having It All' and Russian Roulette 151
35. Crossing a Finish Line 156
36. Emilia Finds Some Words 158
37. Finding Intimations of the Possible in a Well-
    Formed Ankle and a Polka-Dotted Cravat 163
Afterword 166
Acknowledgements 173

FOREWORD

Many high school students are frustrated by their inability to articulate the serious concerns they think about. They fear that having such concerns stigmatizes them as aberrations. This book is for them. *Letters of Recommendation* affirms the idea that to be young is to be enthralled by life's most serious questions: What is my purpose? What matters? How should I live my life? I have written this book to reassure a young person that to claim those questions as hers is the first step towards achieving her adult self. My means of doing this is by illuminating the emergence of the inner life of a seventeen-year-old girl.

Many teachers are frustrated by the persistent and pervasive stigma, best summed up by the phrase, "those who can, do; those who can't, teach." This attitude is doubly pernicious; it denigrates teaching both as a part of everyone's life and as a vocation to which some persons dedicate their lives. It misguides the public. It narrows the place of education into a scorned ghetto, and it invites efforts to save instruction from teachers, presumed to be incompetent, through fixed methods and packaged curricula.

Young persons engage in continuous self-formation. Alert to what surrounds them, they make teachers of everyone, and engage some as teachers by mission and profession. This book is for the teacher in each of us and especially for those who make teaching central to their life work. *Letters of Recommendation* affirms teaching as an active art. As teachers, we respond to the young, developing with them the skills and desires for lives of shared meaning and worth, thereby constantly renewing the culture's legacy and fortifying the values associated with living a civilized life. I cannot think of a more demanding and significant calling.

We first meet Emilia Carlyle, a senior at an elite private school in New York City; through a letter she has written to Doc, her history teacher. Although Emilia is a high school senior, the issues she and Doc explore are those that thoughtful young people continue to confront in college and into young adulthood, particularly as they establish careers. Previously, Emilia had asked Doc to write a letter of recommendation for her early admission to Harvard. The apparent reason she sends the follow up letter is to inform Doc that she has decided not to apply early. Emilia has not been able to draft her college essay; consequently her application will not be completed by the November 1 deadline.

As Doc reads Emilia's letter it becomes evident that Emilia is troubled. The college admissions process itself troubles her, but more significantly, she is troubled by the questions it raises about the purpose of education and its relation to living a good life. Doc suggests that they explore those questions in a series of letters.

Emilia and Doc exchange their letters over the course of Emilia's senior year. The catalyst for their reflections is daily life at Alden, the school Emilia attends and where Doc teaches. Amidst all the frenetic activity that characterizes Emilia's world her inner life begins to emerge. That emergence is premised on Emilia's taking responsibility for her education as she comes to understand education as a process of self-formation. Emilia's inner life emerges as she develops capacities that will enable her to discover and to achieve her purpose.

Although initially unable to articulate it, Emilia's discontent about her education is rooted in a disconnect she feels between her instruction at school and her experience outside of the classroom. *Letters of Recommendation* serves as a means to address this disconnect. I do this by imagining an exchange of rather formal letters, anachronistic in this age of email and texting. I use the letters as a way of focusing our attention on personal concerns and developments that ordinarily take place in a person's subjective, internal dialogue and become manifest only in a jumble of interactions mediated in a variety of ways. Because I want to display complex inner developments clearly, I usually have both Emilia and Doc express themselves with a more formal, precise diction than students and teachers would use in their everyday encounters. Although I use the letters here as a literary means to distill and express what I have learned through diverse experiences, I suspect that an actual exchange of letters between a student and a teacher might, on occasion, prove to be a reflective pedagogy in a time in which personal interactions tend to be instantaneous and prefabricated.

Here, within the book, the letters between Emilia and Doc express the halting yet necessary steps by which a person takes responsibility for her education and inner life. With this purpose in mind, Doc and Emilia discuss a variety of topics that go beyond the immediate concern of being admitted to Harvard. Over the course of the year they discuss the differences between schooling and achieving an education, between study and instruction, between knowledge as a means and knowledge as an end, between success and fulfillment, as well as the relationship between the ideal, the real, and the actual. Emilia's friendship with Lilly, Luis and Caleb gives these discussions context and significance. During her second semester, Emilia recognizes these differences while reading William James for an independent study project. In addition she begins to reflect on the reciprocal relationship between the self and society. She ponders the connection between cultivating her character and fulfilling her role as citizen.

Having spent the bulk of my adult life in the company of adolescents, teaching those who are privileged and those who are not, it is clear that youth of all backgrounds have an inner life that neither they nor their observers normally perceive in its fullness. I have come to understand that adolescents lead a double life: their public and private selves are often in tension with one another.

In Emilia's case her public persona, privileged and precocious beyond her years, appears to set her apart from her peers. Few high school seniors would choose to read William James or spend their free time analyzing the meaning of their educations. Even though those activities are peculiar to Emilia, the reason she chooses them is one she holds in common with the broad spectrum of her peers. Reading William James and writing to Doc are the means Emilia employs to discover, to think about, and to articulate her purpose. Emilia might be imaginary, but I would argue her desire to do this, to cultivate her inner life, is the work she shares with every other adolescent and young adult. Jean-Jacques Rousseau described the achievement of this work as a person's second birth.

Over the years I have observed my students acting as midwives to themselves. I have come to appreciate the variety of means they choose to go about their work. Their means are as varied as they are. Some, like Emilia, will choose activities that challenge and stretch their critical and analytical capabilities. Others will shape their inner lives by perfecting athletic, mathematical, imaginative, entrepreneurial, comedic, mechanical, moral, artistic, linguistic, musical, scientific, or social capabilities. Then there are those adolescents and young adults who choose means that initiate an odyssey of self-destruction—a journey, democratic in its allure, capable of seducing trust-fund scions, the girls and boys next door, and the dispossessed. The resulting addiction, despair, violence and death bear witness to youthful purposes thwarted and inner lives stillborn.

For a young person, the desire to find her purpose necessitates crafting an inner life. That work is sparked by an intimation and an imperative. The intimation suggests that what is labeled reality is not all there is. The imperative challenges the young to test the limits of what is and to discover what is possible. To act on this intimation and fulfill this imperative a young person must look to her own experience as an educative force. This is difficult. Like Emilia, many adolescents feel a disconnect between their schooling and their experience owing to a fundamental misperception. They, like most of the population, conflate the definition of education with schooling, and instruction with study. This misperception causes the young to mistrust, even in some cases to discount, their own experience as an educative force.

Emilia becomes aware of this perceptual blindness while

serving as a student representative on Alden's Curriculum Committee. When she asks herself what educates, she sees what has always been in plain sight: the city has been one of her most important educators. Inspired by that insight, Emilia initiates a campaign to persuade the Curriculum Committee to make Doc's *City as Educator* project the official curriculum for Alden's second semester seniors. Although events do not unfold according to plan, Emilia nevertheless undergoes a formative experience. Doc supports and sustains that self-formation without presuming to determine it, a difficult art.

In representing both the student's self-formation and a teacher's sustaining responses, I have refrained from spicing the story with crises and emotional turmoil. A self in formation may find her life course riven by catastrophe, but the self-forming goes on within the everyday life that preceded and follows it. Teachers may at times be drawn into parenting, crisis management, healing, and therapy, but at the cost of putting their art as a teacher aside. *Letters of Recommendation* addresses self-formation and teaching, central concerns in life, but not the whole of life for either teacher or student. Writing to her teacher, a person she chooses to respect, Emilia naturally seeks recognition as a person capable of serious reflection. Doc understands this. She knows that if she is to help Emilia think about what matters, she must assume the role of guide, neither friend nor parent. Consequently she is always conscious of maintaining emotional space between Emilia and herself.

Finally, Emilia is a child of modest privilege in a world steeped in its extremes. Hence, *Letters of Recommendation* engages a contentious issue central to the current debates about education. Aside from discussions about implementing strategies for producing high test scores, making teachers accountable, and the number of dollars allocated per pupil, little is said about the tone, the quality of interaction needed in a school to make excellence in education possible. Having Emilia attend a school like Alden where student achievement, teacher accountability, and abundant resources are not wanting, gives me the opportunity to concentrate on these matters of *tone*, to illuminate how excellence is really woven into the daily lives of a student and her teacher.

It is not that the subtleties of excellent self-formation are unique to schools like Alden, but they are perhaps more visible there because the intrusion of external constraints is less imperious. Even with constraints in abeyance, failure and mediocrity are too often the result, but the actual process of self-formation, and the quality of teaching that supports it, may more easily be observed. And readers should recognize my using an imagined exchange of letters to promote reflection on what takes place in the interaction of students and teachers as a literary device, not a suggested instructional method.

In the realities of an excellent education, a student nurturing herself and a teacher providing stimulus and support interact as distinctive, mutually responsible persons. In doing so, they become for each other examples of the cultural legacies that they join to preserve and advance. Breaking 2250 on the SAT may be important, but it is an incidental side effect of real education. And real education can take place without the conventional badges of educational success, and vice versa. Having Emilia attend a school like Alden also gives us the opportunity to think about the flip side of the excellence question, one largely ignored: What happens when good instruction takes place without real education? How does that combination affect the commonweal?

In sum, I hope *Letters of Recommendation* will be read as both a radical and a conservative book. The book intends to be radical in the sense that it portrays our current fixation on the instrumental interpretation of education, to the exclusion of others, as ill timed at best and self-defeating in most cases. In attempting to transform a young person into a skilled worker, an accomplished product, a savvy consumer, or a cosmopolitan citizen, a predominately instrumental education transforms her into a means to meet extrinsic ends, all before she has figured out what her ends can and should be. But *Letters of Recommendation* is also a conservative book in that it aims to broaden our interpretation of education by resurrecting an old idea. If at the core of our understanding of what it means to live a human life is the commitment to recognizing persons as ends in themselves, then education must do no less than affirm that ideal.

TO MY STUDENTS AND COLLEAGUES

1. Emilia Starts the School Year with Writer's Block and Second Thoughts

October 3

Dear Doc,

What a mistake! A few days ago I told you I was applying early to Harvard and asked if you would write a recommendation. Although I still want you to write on my behalf, I won't be applying early to Harvard or anywhere else. Throughout the summer I was confident I could have my application ready to send out by November 1. That way the college process would be off my back as quickly as possible. I've come to realize that's an unrealistic goal because I overestimated my ability to juggle this semester's commitments: course work, the application process, the soccer team, the Curriculum Committee, SAT prep, and maintaining a social life.

So the good news for both of us is we have more time. Although time was a huge factor in my decision not to apply early, it wasn't the most important one. Quite frankly Doc, I'm starting to wonder why go to college in the first place. That question has made it difficult for me to complete my application in time for the early decision deadline. Specifically I'm having trouble drafting my college essay.

What's weird is I love to write and up until now have never experienced writer's block. Needless to say it couldn't have come at a worse time. I know this sounds crazy, but instead of writing to the various admissions committees explaining the unique qualities I would bring to their freshman class, I'd like to ask each committee one simple question: What unique contribution will their college make to the Emilia Carlyle story? What I don't understand is why, now, when the pressure is on, do I have this urge to blow my chances of being accepted anywhere?

Believe me, I'm as surprised as anyone that I'm having second thoughts about applying to college. Growing up, I simply assumed going to college was as inevitable as getting taller. The only uncertainty was which one I would attend. Since college was a given, my family, friends, teachers, and I never saw the need to spell out reasons for going. Does a person make explicit her reasons for eating or sleeping? For me an unanticipated repercussion of the admissions process, or what I call the college sweepstakes, has been the need to state those reasons and examine whether they are valid. Over the past several weeks I've come to recognize the unspoken understanding that has made college a fact of life for me. I thought I needed college to define who I am. Now, I'm wondering whether that's the case.

I am unloading all of this on you because I think you will understand my sudden ambivalence. My hunch is based on a situation that arose last year. It was the first week of April and you started class with some tips about writing the research paper that was due in May. It was also the week seniors who had not applied early learned their fates. Even though the class was made up of all juniors, we were preoccupied with tracking which senior got into what school. In most cases our interest had little to do with the people involved. Our interest was self-interest. My classmates and I were searching for clues, trying to identify patterns, dreaming of devising algorithms—anything that would reveal the qualities which made one applicant acceptable and another not.

Even as juniors many of us were having second thoughts about the admissions process, doubting whether it was the rational process it appeared to be. Rational in the sense that it was a process we could count on to deliver predictable and generally favorable results. But then there was the inexplicable: colleges rejecting or wait-listing seniors we considered well qualified. Equally unsettling was hearing that those same colleges accepted seniors we thought didn't deserve to get in. As juniors we were already beginning to come to grips with the possibility that the admissions process was more like a mysterious rite of passage, its outcomes determined by forces unknown to us and out of our control. Fortunately as juniors we still had enough trust and faith in the process to shake off such a disturbing thought.

The admission process's procedures and timetables reassured us that doubting the reasonableness of the process was itself unreasonable. Since it was April, my classmates and I were already busy making individual and family appointments with the college counselors, preparing to take the first round of SATs and APs, and making plans to visit colleges over the summer. We clung to the belief that owing to years of dedicating ourselves to becoming the best applicants possible we deserved to be admitted among the chosen.

That was what many of us had on our minds that day in April when you started to discuss the research paper. For me that day was memorable. Instead of denying or bemoaning our distracted state you addressed it. I think I can safely say that for everyone in the class it was probably the first and only time an academic teacher took class time to talk about the significance of the college process. Do you remember what you said? The gist of it was that we have little control over whether college X accepts or rejects us. That decision will be determined by the mix of qualities college X's admissions committee is seeking for the purpose of shaping its freshman class. What we do control is whether college X's acceptance or rejection becomes a measure of our worth.

Boy did that hit home! As a junior I watched my friends who were seniors do exactly what you warned against. They got so caught up in the process that it seemed the very idea of who they were depended on where they went. The blowback from this was terrible. I knew two seniors, friends since sixth grade, who applied early to the same school. One was accepted and the other rejected. The friendship withered due to the resentment and envy the friend who wasn't admitted felt towards the one that was. Observing this, I was determined to follow your advice. I promised myself not to allow a college's acceptance or rejection to become a judgment about who I am. It took only two months for that promise to begin to unravel.

3

And to make matters worse, I began losing my perspective in a place I thought of as a refuge for maintaining it.

Since I was nine I've attended a sleep away camp that I love. Although the camp is dedicated to the arts, it's not a creative boot camp. As a camper I had a lot of freedom to choose what I wanted to do and when to do it. If one day my playwriting buddies and I wanted to work all afternoon, we did. If the next day we decided to spend most of the afternoon swimming so be it, just as long as the play was ready to be performed on the assigned date. I loved it there because it was the one place I was encouraged to experiment rather than worry about being perfect. Although I initially went to this camp to take advantage of its drama program, I probably ended up spending as much time weaving as I did writing, directing and acting. The camp was my great escape: a place to get away from parents, school pressures, city routines, and city friends.

This past summer I was looking forward to returning as a C.I.T. But the release the camp had always provided didn't happen. Physically I was located in the Adirondacks but mentally I was here, thinking about my classmates who had already visited all the colleges on their lists and had completed drafting their application essays. And then there were those classmates of mine, summering all over the globe, perfecting their language skills under the tutelage of a family of native speakers. And if the thought of my halting Spanish wasn't enough to make me anxious there was always the image of my more civic-minded peers braving exhaustion and disease to erect houses somewhere in Central America.

When I returned to the city, about two weeks before school started, it was apparent that the college sweepstakes was underway and the competition fierce. A number of my classmates had finished filling in their applications and had gone on to the next step—figuring out which teacher to ask for a recommendation. Even before school opened, SAT tutors and application consultants were hired. Supposedly these consultants know how to put together an application packet that will be even more outstanding than you are. The scrambling, the strategizing, the obsessing all for a handful of places at a handful of schools, it's the senior year version of survival of the fittest. For all the talk about community, mutual respect, and moral courage that goes on in a school like Alden, when push comes to shove it's each student out for him or herself.

What did I take away from all of this? I think education has nothing to do with how to live except for learning how to package yourself for success. Who cares whether the number of extracurricular activities you've listed on your application is inflated or not? Why lose sleep over your motivation for doing community service? No one needs to know that you do it only to appear civic minded, when in reality you couldn't care less. It's tough out there and everyone has to maintain an edge to succeed. We get the message! It's not pretty and maybe not right, but in the real world that's what an education is for. By the time a student graduates from Alden she has learned that being the first and the best is really what matters. As I see it, the most important advantage an excellent education provides is simply to appear to have left the rest of the pack behind.

Doc, to say I am confused about what I've been learning for the last fourteen years is an understatement. I hope you will understand and not dismiss what I've written as an adolescent tantrum thrown by a spoiled drama queen. On the one hand, I've done well at an excellent school and chances are the success I have known will continue. What more could a person want? On the other hand, I feel what I've learned over these years has had little to do with who I am or want to be. I would really like to understand this disconnect.

2. Doc Offers a Not-So-Modest Proposal

Dear Emilia,

I was both thankful and concerned after reading your letter. Thankful for having more time to write your recommendation and concerned by the issues it raises. That said, let me deal with the simplest issue first. If it's any consolation I also feel as if I've been shot out of a cannon at the start of the school year. Like you, I attribute much of my September frenzy to performing a balancing act—trying to meet the deadlines imposed by the admissions process while responding to the real time demands of starting the school year.

Even though the school's college counselors have designated October the start of open season for recommendation requests, that date holds as much weight as the Friday after Thanksgiving does for designating the start of the holiday shopping season. By the end of the first week of school I have already agreed to write recommendations for seniors applying early. All of this is occurring while I'm trying to learn the names of the juniors in my American history classes. Unlike you, though, I can count on experience to help me resist feelings of becoming overwhelmed. I take comfort in the fact that I've performed this balancing act many times before. That recognition enables me to trust that my students will not go through the year nameless and the recommendations will get written in good time.

As to your other concern, the disconnect you feel between what you've learned as a student and what you need to know in order to become the person you aspire to be, that concern deserves sustained and mindful reflection. It raises difficult questions about the relationship between a person's sense of self, her purpose, and her education. I think that particularly at your stage of life, puzzling out who you might become is inexorably linked to discovering what your purposes might be. My hunch is that the disconnect you mentioned is rooted in your perception that the education you've received has contributed little to that end. If we are serious about exploring that disconnect then we will need to marshal the time and energy to examine how an education forms a self.

Let me assure you that questions of identity present a daunting challenge even for those of us who are well past adolescence. "Know thyself," as the ancient oracle instructed requires a lifetime of steps and miss steps. Knowing another is even more difficult. To think that I'm able to comprehend another person who I intermittently encounter is both presumptuous and foolish.

When it comes to you, I plead guilty on both counts. The fundamental error I made was to presume there existed a seamless match between your inner and outer self—between your private and public life. Having devoted most of my adult life to teaching adolescents, I should have known better. Relying on public benchmarks—academic record, social poise, and athletic prowess—I assumed the college admissions process presented nothing more than another rung on the meritocratic ladder for you; one you would adroitly climb. The possibility that your inner self might be questioning the process never entered my mind.

So imagine my surprise when a person I had consigned to the winner category in that process delivered one of the most scathing critiques of education I had ever heard from someone your age. Although you credited Alden for the excellent job it did in preparing you academically, you condemned its apparent hypocrisy. All the talk that goes on here about living nobly, giving back, and keeping to the highest moral standards you see as nothing more than a smoke screen, making it easier for you and your classmates to satisfy your own self-interest. Hurt, rage, and betrayal punctuated that observation, but who betrayed you? Teachers? Peers? Administrators? Yourself?

At first your assessment of the education you've received

put me on the defensive. If not directly responsible for culti-vating the cynicism and narcissism your portrayal elicited, wasn't I, as a teacher at Alden, complicit in creating the condi-tions that nurtured it? Maybe, I thought, the best way to chal-lenge your interpretation of education's purpose was to pro-vide you with a reality check, something along the lines of the following:

"Look Emilia," I would say, "welcome to the world most of us inhabit—where there isn't enough to go around and the struggle for getting your share usually brings out the worst in people. In your case we're talking about early acceptance to an elite college, not life's basics like food, clothing, shelter, medi-cine, a job, and yes, a chance to go to school, all that prosaic stuff most of us spend our lives securing. So let's cut the whin-ing. We're not talking survival here, we're talking about whether or not you'll spend the next four years at an ivy league school, a baby ivy, or an honors program in one of the country's premier state universities."

Why didn't I say this to you? Rereading your letter made it clear that you did not need a reality check. Shocking you into the real is not the issue. No, the issue is one of helping to un-pack a reality you are struggling to understand, a reality far more complex than a case of the college admissions blues.

This brings me to a proposal. Would you be interested in exploring an alternative to the interpretation of education you articulated through an exchange of letters? Even in the age of twitter and texting, I find this archaic form of communication has its charms: it offers a more leisured pace and expansive canvas on which to write. I think a different perspective is what you are seeking. Otherwise why would equating educa-tion with packaging oneself for success unnerve you so?

My hunch is you want to believe that there is more to be-coming educated than being admitted early to Harvard. I would like to think of this exchange of letters as a means of providing grounds for that belief. To state the obvious, com-posing the letters will demand a commitment of time and en-ergy that neither of us has in abundance. But if the project has meaning for you, those constraints can be overcome. Let me know what you decide.

3.　Emilia Regards Teachers as Persons of Interest

Dear Doc,

I'm in. For obvious reasons education has become a hot topic for me lately. Along with playing college admissions sweepstakes, I'm one of the student representatives serving on the Curriculum Committee. So your proposal came at the right time. Who knows maybe our letters will transform the thoughts I have into the college essay I need to write. Maybe writing these letters will help me come up with ideas to present to the Committee.

The Committee had its first meeting last Thursday. It was devoted to laying out the agenda for the year. Topping its "to do" list was developing strategies to prevent second semester seniors from slacking off. Although most of the members thought requiring seniors to take final exams would solve the problem, I suggested looking into internship programs and offering more opportunities for independent study. Everyone around the table listened politely, but I got the impression my suggestions were summarily dismissed as impractical and just a kid spouting off.

Nothing was decided, but we were told that the headmaster considers the senior year a priority and an issue we will revisit during subsequent meetings. It seems unlikely a major change will happen this year. Even though second semester might not be any different for my graduating class, I still want to propose a plan that would offer future seniors something more than the experience of muddling through from February to May. Unfortunately, except for a half-baked notion about internships I don't have a clue what that might be.

What I do know is that walking home after the meeting I felt disappointed because I realized that change is a slow and drawn out process at Alden. Even after two years of discussion, a decision that appears relatively simple should there be three or four years of required history, has yet to be made. That being said, I take my role as a Committee member seriously.

I suppose my classmates nominated me because they know I'm not shy about criticizing school policies that I think are misguided. Now as a member of the Curriculum Committee I have the chance to turn talk into action. Last spring, after the Committee's final meeting, I asked Jordan if she had any tips to help me become an effective member. She advised that whenever I present an idea to back it up with a detailed plan. According to her, the plan is necessary because it demonstrates that I've thought the idea through and the Committee will be more likely to consider it.

As much as I criticize Alden, I have to say the administration and the faculty did the right thing when they allowed students to become Curriculum Committee members. It's always struck me as crazy that students are rarely consulted when education is discussed. It seems a no-brainer to me. A person who has spent thirteen of her seventeen years in school should have a pretty good idea of what works and what doesn't. Among all the talking heads pontificating about education these days, no one I can think of represents the views of those of us under twenty. Adults probably assume teenagers are too self-involved to care about complex educational issues. On those rare occasions when we do show interest, they think it is to decide questions that require no more thought than where to have the prom. But adults underestimate us.

Spending a year preoccupied with the college process, my friends and I don't do much else but think about education. Even before we got caught up in the college frenzy, we spent a lot of time talking about teachers. I wonder whether teachers are aware of the impact they make on students that goes beyond their role. Even though we know they were young once, my friends and I have a difficult time imagining any of them as middle school outcasts, confused high school seniors, or stressed out college sophomores. When we discuss teachers it's their back-stories we try to fill in, piecing those stories together from the little my friends and I know about their lives outside the classroom.

We do that because we want to know why they decided to dedicate themselves to algorithms, dangling participles, or in your case, Andrew Jackson's bank phobia. Does it ever dawn on teachers that the kids who are their captive audience for as much as five days a week for ten months a year would like to know why they decided to do what they do? When did Mr. Thompson realize life was good as long as calculus was part of it? When did Ms. Basso find physics so riveting that she couldn't wait to spread the word about entropy? When did Doc O' Riley's love of poetry become so intense that he believes a person who hasn't memorized a poem can't lead a fully human life? What caused these teachers to develop a passion for what they do? How do they manage to sustain it over the years?

Now that I'm wondering what to do with my life, hearing my teachers' stories is important. I realize there's a professional line teachers can't and shouldn't cross when it comes to telling students details about their personal lives. Believe me the last thing I want to hear about is the erotic life of my Latin teacher. What I and many of my peers would welcome is to hear our teachers talk about how they made key decisions in their lives. By the time a student is ready to graduate high school, it's inspiring and reassuring to listen to a respected teacher's account of what it took to become an adult capable of bringing feeling to what she thinks, thought to what she feels, and passion to what she does.

When a teacher is passionate about her work there's something distinctive about the way she does it. Doc, are you aware you have a particular way of standing that signals you are ready to attack a gross generalization or mistaken assumption? Your students call it the Pounce. You stand as if you just took a hit in the stomach with one hand covering your mouth and the other arm across your waist. Next, you remove the hand covering your mouth and extend it forward as if you are grabbing the misguided opinion out of the air. Then you ask a question

12

that explodes it. Believe me, the Pounce's story is one I'd like to hear.

4. What Are We Talking About When We Talk About Education?

Dear Emilia,

The Pounce? I wish I had an intriguing story to tell, but until you brought it up I was unaware of having a distinctive set of teaching moves. Gauging by the laughter and applause Megan's impersonation evoked at the Halloween Assembly, my obliviousness was not shared. I suppose the Pounce is one of those personal quirks that just developed over time. Who knows, it might have originated when, as a girl, I briefly considered studying ballet as a profession. Maybe the Pounce is my inner dancer trying to get out.

Watching the Halloween Assembly, I thought about your question, whether or not the faculty is aware of the impact they make on students. How could they not be? The senior class's tradition of dressing up as particular faculty members and then putting on a skit that satirizes their idiosyncrasies makes it clear that Alden students perceive many of their teachers as more than the role. At the high school I attended, such displays of wit would be perceived as disrespect for the role and would elicit a visit to the principal's office. Rereading your letter, I wondered if there was a quality the teachers you admired had in common—a quality that made students want to know them better. Actually you described it. Towards the end of the letter you wrote about teachers who " . . . bring feeling to what they think, thought to what they feel, and passion to what they do." I call that integrity.

The teachers you mentioned exemplify integrity: they use what they know to ground who they are and how they act. These days, I think integrity is becoming an increasingly rare character trait. Many adults in public life take pride in their ability to compartmentalize, to separate who they are, from what they know, and what they know from the deeds they do.

I worry that young people steeped in this ethos will imagine that becoming an adult requires no more than using any means necessary to get what they want and marshaling enough cunning to evade responsibility when their machinations turn sour. Those conditions are the breeding ground for nihilism, a terrifying state of mind where anything is possible.

I suspect that what you mean by finding out the back-story about a teacher is to hear his account of the decision making process that enabled him to cultivate a sense of integrity. Why not ask about it? If there's one quality you and most Alden students do not suffer from its social awkwardness. Starting in the Lower School students are encouraged to interact with people in authority, to learn what is appropriate behavior, to listen to their stories, and to share their own. It isn't as if teachers at Alden are unapproachable. Consider the opportunities—free periods, after school, even during lunch—when you could sit down with a teacher and find out more about him. It's a matter of taking the initiative and finding the right time. If you can handle a college interview, what's so intimidating about asking a person why teaching became his vocation?

What's interesting about the relationship between integrity and the teachers you admire is that it casts doubt on your description of education. If, as you assert, education is learning how to package yourself for success, then how do you explain Ms. Basso, Mr. Thompson, or Doc O' Riley? To make my point even clearer, get out your student handbook and turn to the page that lists the faculty and their educational backgrounds. You will find that all three graduated from the best colleges and went on to earn advanced degrees. If, as you conclude, education is nothing more than learning how to run the rat race better than the next person, then why did these people choose to dedicate themselves to a profession that earns little public esteem and even less money? Either there is something missing from your description of education, or they're really losers even though you were fooled into thinking otherwise, perhaps owing to your youth and inexperience. I think you will agree, that we can readily dismiss the second alternative.

From what I observe, adolescents are masters at detecting a phony and you're no exception. The teachers you admire are the real deal, so let's get to the heart of the matter and ask what are we talking about when we talk about education?

You would think that's an easy question to answer, but when listening to conversations about education it becomes apparent that's not the case. The difficulty arises because people don't distinguish between getting schooled and becoming educated. Another and shorter way of saying the same thing is that they conflate schooling with education. The effect of using these two phrases interchangeably is to spread and promote the erroneous impression that being a student and aspiring to become an educated person are one and the same undertaking. In other words the very language we rely on to think about and communicate our thoughts about education leads us to equate the part or the means, fulfilling the role of student, with the whole or the end, aspiring to become an educated person.

How would I describe education? I would describe it as the project a person undertakes to form her inner life by developing capacities that enable her to recognize and to achieve her purpose. The inner life I have in mind is that continuous dialogue a person has with herself. It's the dialogue only she hears, the one which judges, counsels, cajoles, condemns, and commends her acting in the world.

What I think is missing from your description of education is agency. A person acting as an agent takes responsibility for choosing her purposes. By choosing, a person changes the meaning of education from a set of operations working on her to a project she undertakes; she becomes her education's active agent rather than its passive recipient. You assert that "packaging oneself for success is education's purpose," I disagree.

Packaging, although it generates a lot of activity and effort, is a passive response to others' values. By packaging herself, a person might believe she's taking responsibility for her own best interests, but because the choices she makes are limited to options others have deemed success worthy, that's an illusion. Think about the conflict you're having with yourself about the

16

college essay. Why won't you write the essay you really want to? The one that would ask the various admissions committees what unique contribution their respective colleges would make to your ability to form yourself? Simple—you fear that the committees would perceive the question as inappropriate, if not impertinent, and your chances of being accepted would suffer.

Success—whether it entails getting accepted to the right school or becoming fabulously rich—is a means not a purpose or end because it must point beyond itself in order to have meaning. Success begs the question. Success for what? Success for power, wealth, celebrity, security? An end, on the other hand, is what it says it is. It represents the point in a person's inner dialogue when she stops deliberating about why she should act one way or another, or not at all.

A multiplicity of resources is required if a person's purpose is to emerge from her inner dialogue. Among these resources are facts, questions, concepts, theories, feelings, metaphors, formulas, beliefs, symbols, signs, aspirations, ideals and judgments. All constitute the inner dialogue's language. I particularly want to attend to two types of questions that are basic to a person's inner life. I think confusion about them feeds your disillusion with your own education. The first question asks, how do I do X? The second asks, why should I do it? The first is a question about means. The second is a question about ends or purposes. An educated person takes responsibility for asking both, as well as for judging whether the means she chooses are appropriate for the purposes she aspires to achieve.

I think your disillusion about your education is caused by confusion about the relationship between schooling and those two types of questions, between means and ends. It stems from the problem of conflating schooling with education that I mentioned earlier. You have mistakenly made schooling an end in itself instead of a means to pursuing an education, and you are far from alone. It's a confusion that pulsates throughout our culture.

This misunderstanding spawned and sustains your feeling

of betrayal by Alden. Somehow the school is perpetrating a bait and switch con. The bait is the school's professed mission to foster an inquiring spirit in its students. That's the end Alden professes it will provide its students—preparing each to embrace future questions of ends with vigor, imagination, and a sense of possibility unique to him or her. The switch consists of using that spirit not to give shape and substance to a student's inner life, but to crank out individuals who are fast, efficient, and facile at analyzing and critiquing everything and everyone but themselves. Towards that end students are taught to discuss and to write on topics ranging from Huck Finn's moral dilemma to Einstein and Bohr's debates about quantum mechanics. In other words, the school takes an end, an inquiring spirit, and transforms it into a means for producing successful products, products that will have no problem collecting society's glittering prizes.

That's the hypocrisy you accuse the school of practicing. But your accusation is unfair because you level it under the sway of a misconception, that schooling and education are one and the same, which is to say you mistake the means for the end. Owing to this confusion, you shift the responsibility for choosing your ends onto Alden instead of taking the responsibility yourself. Doing so you cede to others the authority to determine your purpose.

This relinquishing of authority is not the outcome of a co-ordinated assault by the school on your autonomy. At best all Alden can do is provide the content, skills, and contacts that sustain and guide the explorations a person undertakes to achieve her ends. In that respect you are extraordinarily fortunate. The instruction a student receives at a school like ours offers a stunning variety of resources to support that endeavor. Alden has the resources, cultural, human, and financial, to provide its students with a cornucopia of examples that illuminate the languages others have used to form themselves. Over time those languages have been incorporated into a cultural voice. During any given week at Alden, you might have the good fortune to investigate Toni Morrison's, Suleiman's,

Desmond Tutu's, Emma Goodman's, Lorca's, Mao's, Madame Curie's, Einstein's, Picasso's, Virgil's, John Coltrane's or Shakespeare's attempts to communicate what matters.

You are mistaken to think a conspiracy fomented by Alden seduces a student into relinquishing her responsibility for articulating and achieving her ends. No, escaping from forming oneself is the consequence of a slow and incremental addiction. It is the effect of becoming habituated to the questions our can-do society embraces and rewards, questions about how to accomplish X. The allure these questions proffer is both simple and potent; the better your ability to answer them the greater your success.

Take a minute and think of all the activity that goes on in school that is generated by the word "how": how to write an essay, how to solve for X, how to conduct the experiment, how to make the jump shot, how to refine the sketch, how to recognize the subjunctive case. How questions are the lifeblood of a school because they provide an opportunity for you, as student, to demonstrate your mastery of the skills and content that will result in a correct answer.

In the larger society the same can be said for an adult in her role as worker. Now there are several assumptions at play here. First, the "how-question" has content and a method that will lead to a correct answer. Second, there is a consensus about what that answer is. Third, you can be objectively evaluated as to whether or not you achieve the answer. Fourth, you will be rewarded commensurate with your performance. The type of question that schools and society embrace has as its purpose meeting standards, realizing goals, and gaining tangible rewards, three fundamentals a can-do culture relies on for keeping busy and getting things done.

As much as a can-do culture loves the how-question, it demonstrates little love for questions of ends. A person reflecting on the meaning of what she's doing is suspect. Indeed if this practice were to spread throughout a population, it could derail the ceaseless activity that is our culture's source of self-definition and pride. Instead of focusing on how to do X, she and others like her, would waste time asking why do X in the first place?

To make matters worse these questions are also potentially subversive. Since they are the building blocks of a person's inner life and therefore intensively private, questions of ends emerge unconstrained by the usual means of societal control. Who knows where that can lead? It might lead to imagining new possibilities that undermine the status quo. Unlike the questions that ask how, there is no method or content that can be taught to answer why. Answers cannot be objectively evaluated because there's no consensus about what a correct answer to questions that ask why should be. Since there's no consensus about the correct answer there's no extrinsic reward attached to these questions. I had an Uncle Walt who called questions about why, "navel gazing." For him contemplating why was a complete waste of time, energy, and money. If Walt were alive when "just do it" became a well-advertised commandment, he, like millions of others, would consider that slogan as words to live by.

So why bother? Why knock yourself out about questions of ends? It's pretty obvious that a person can lead a successful life without dealing with any of it. In fact considering how culturally suspect these questions are, it's probably the case that a person is better off without them. Let's face it, these questions demand intense, long lasting, and demanding study that is self-directed. No one is going to teach you to figure out your purpose. There is no ready-made course you can take. There are no answers to discover in the back of the book because the book hasn't been written. It's all your responsibility—the questions, the study, the answers—all created out of your own experience.

And if that's not enough to dampen your enthusiasm for questions of ends, there's the double life. Given our society's deep ambivalence about them, if you take these questions seriously you'll be forced to conduct your study largely under the cover of a more conventional role. It's likely that in the course of leading a double life you will become critical of much of what passes as reality. You'll find yourself becoming incensed by what most people choose to ignore because "that's just the way things are."

Although critical thinking is the skill everyone in school claims to respect, the claim is at best an illusion. Once enclosed in an institution, critical thinking, like questions about ends is co-opted; its purpose restricted. You're encouraged to think critically as long as it's about the means to achieve the correct answer, but not about the question itself. If that were to happen then we would be getting into why territory and there's no telling where that will lead. If you choose to think critically about ends don't expect to be applauded for your effort in school or out. If people listen to what you have to say, more than likely they will not hear its substance and will wonder why you have such a negative attitude about everything.

So where does all of this leave you? Up against it. Over the next four years situations will arise that will cause you to decide whether you want to think about your purpose or take a pass. Sure you can live a successful life, even an accomplished one, without thinking about ends, but at a price. The defining feature of that life will be a continual progression of functions you will have to perform. Why? By lifting the responsibility of pursuing questions of ends from your shoulders you give others the authority to define your purpose. In effect your inner voice will become an echo chamber filled with the thoughts that others voice.

This brings me back to the disconnect you feel between what you know and who you want to become. That unnerving sensation is the consequence of perceiving yourself as a means to others' ends. Whether you call the disconnect self-alienation or give it a more positive spin and label it compartmentalization, it's the antithesis of the integrity you admire. Rest assured if, allowed to define who you are, over time, the disconnect will make it impossible for you to cultivate a sense of integrity within yourself. And just as the disconnect destabilizes your inner life it does the same to your public self. Without a sense of purpose of your own, you're vulnerable to every form of manipulation that's out there. Isn't that exactly how you don't want to live?

5. Emilia Rereads Randolph Bourne's Essay and Writes One of Her Own

November 7

Dear Doc,

I've been pounced! I have to admit my description of education was just a wee bit narrow, more of a rant than a description. Along with showing me the error of my ways the pouncing served another purpose. It shed light on something that has been on my mind since last year. It started when you assigned *Twilight of Idols*. I have to tell you Doc, *Twilight of Idols* unhinged me. This might sound weird, but when I read it last spring I had the feeling that Randolph Bourne could be describing my life, even though he was criticizing American intellectuals and their support for this country's entry into World War 1. Until now, I couldn't explain why I felt that way. What does Bourne's argument against intellectuals living in 1917 have to do with me, a high school student living at the start of the 21st century?

Twilight became personal when I read the following passage: "His [Dewey's] disciples have learned all too literally the instrumental attitude toward life, and, being immensely intelligent and energetic, they are making themselves efficient instruments of the war technique, accepting with little question the ends as announced from above. That those ends are largely negative does not concern them, because they have never learned not to subordinate idea to technique. Their education has not given them a coherent system of large ideas, or a feeling for democratic goals. They have, in short, no clear philosophy of life except that of intelligent service, the admirable adaptation of means to ends. They are vague as to what kind of a society they want, or what kind of society America needs, but they are equipped with all the administrative attitudes and talents necessary to attain it."

When I read this passage for the first time, I became so agitated I had to put the essay down and walk around the room several times before I was calm enough to continue. I felt as if Bourne's description of the well educated, or maybe I should say well-schooled youth of his day, could be me and my friends in a few years, but why?

Then I read your letter; ideas began to connect. Now, I can articulate why *Twilight* is as much about my world as it is about America at the start of the twentieth century. When I first read the essay I didn't have a clear understanding of what Bourne meant by the instrumental attitude towards life. After reading your letter I think I'm beginning to get it. An instrumental attitude is what you described as fixating on questions of how—on means—to the exclusion of thinking about questions of why—questions of ends or purposes.

There is another parallel between *Twilight* and your letter. Bourne observed that the education of these young intellectuals provided them with the skills to get things done but no idea why they should do so, except to meet the expectations of those who had authority over them. Finding themselves in that situation, they turn themselves into efficient instruments. Unless I have it wrong, Bourne's observation supports the point you make about needing a purpose of one's own to prevent becoming a means for other people's ends.

I asked myself if I would ever become someone else's efficient instrument. I don't know. What I do know is it doesn't take much for that to happen. Re-reading *Twilight* made that clear. This time I saw how seamlessly success attaches itself to other aspirations. For the youth of Bourne's generation, winning the war became a means to becoming a success, although the intellectuals who supported the war effort would vehemently deny this was the case. They defended their position arguing that winning the war was the means for achieving loftier ends: to make the world safe for democracy, to end all wars, to establish the League of Nations.

Bourne was fighting back and attacked their defense as so much rationalization. He was arguing that the ends they professed were simply platitudes that justified the means they used. OK, today Bourne would call these young intellectuals policy wonks and spin-doctors camouflaging their self-interest as self-sacrificing idealism.

Bourne was observing that intellectuals who supported the war effort made the ends justify the means by adjusting their values to meet immediate demands. They were doing so without questioning whether the means they used to meet those demands would bring about the long-range ends they proclaimed. For Bourne, intellectuals practicing this "philosophy of adjustment" abandoned thinking critically and became apologists for the powerful and the popular, either out of willful blindness or calculated cynicism. Either way the goal was to insure their success.

In your letter you describe the inner life as a dialogue. I think the inner life of the young people Bourne wrote about is better described as a four-step training program. First step: remember you're only as good as what you accomplish. Second step: don't spend time or energy agonizing about what it is you're expected to do. Third step: realize that life is a series of obstacles to overcome. Fourth step: treat obstacles as opportunities to demonstrate your skill and to advance yourself. Even though *Twilight* was written almost a century ago I feel it is about my world. Here I might be making one of those gross generalizations worthy of a pounce, but I think those four steps describe the inner lives of most Alden students, myself included, much of the time. Taken together don't they describe the mindset of an achiever? My friends and I call it clearing the hurdles.

For us clearing the hurdles started early. It started with our parents planning, plotting, and pleading to get us into the right school. For the next twelve years it was a combined effort, on their part and ours, to create a college admissions profile that highlighted our unique talents. Whether that meant attending lacrosse camp, volunteering at dad's friend's genetics lab, or taking cello classes at Juilliard, the point was to transform a personal interest into a skill set that demonstrated initiative, determination, and abilities. It worked. We're the ones admitted early to the college of our choice.

We clear the hurdles, and like Bourne's intellectuals, we do it all in the name of success, the good life, and giving back. The truth is we don't really have ends to call our own beyond making it to the next hurdle faster and more skillfully than anyone else, which becomes an end in itself. You wrote that a person discovers her ends by developing the ongoing dialogue she has with herself. My first reaction was what dialogue? For as long as I can remember my inner voice has spoken the language of hurdle clearing—announcing what I have to do, where I have to be, whom I have to meet and when. You know what I am beginning to suspect about this list of commands? It's a convenient way of denying the possibility that no final hurdle exists because the race has no finish line. That possibility terrifies me.

So what? Here I am, someone lucky enough to have supportive parents, the financial resources, the schooling, the contacts and the capabilities to do just about anything I want, and I'm whining about hurdles. How about all those kids who won't even get a chance to compete in the race? But Bourne's essay suggests there is more to my unease about clearing the hurdles than a privileged schoolgirl experiencing an off day.

If, as my peers and I are repeatedly told we are the leaders of tomorrow, then living a life without thinking about the purpose of what we're doing will have public costs. We'll become leaders who only appear to lead. We will take pride in knowing how to get things done while ignoring whether the means we choose fits the purposes we believe they are fulfilling. Our disregard for the long term consequences of our actions would result in decision makers who believe they are infallible: a belief that is based on nothing more than implementing quick fixes that give the appearance of accomplishment and success.

Doesn't believing that your judgment is infallible lead to "the smartest guys in the room" syndrome and the "we create our own reality" attitude? Confident they can control any contingency, leaders of this sort are unprepared when circumstances prove otherwise. As far as I can tell their fallback position is not to take responsibility for their policies that unravel and to leave it to others to sort out the mess. The messes they create are usually disastrous for the people these leaders are supposed to serve, whether they are victims of a hurricane, soldiers fighting a war, civilians caught in it, a home owner facing foreclosure because his mortgage turned toxic, or a shrimper unable to earn a living because of an oil spill.

Unfortunately, one trait leaders who believe in their own infallibility have in abundance is resilience. When the dust settles, inquiries made, spin spun, they and their stale ideas manage to bounce back rebranded as consultants and talking heads. If this is the type of leader I'm being groomed to be I say thanks but no thanks.

Who knows if I'm cut out to be a leader or not. Right now I'd just be happy to be able to draft my college essay. I'm going to write about Bourne, the hurdles, and finding a purpose. The difficulty will be to keep it to five hundred words. What I'm beginning to understand is it's my call, whether or not college is four more years of hurdle clearing. That being said, I hope wherever I go I'll encounter a person, a situation, a book, an idea that will divert my focus, upend my expectations. That would make it a little easier for me to shore up my courage, take a detour off the straight and narrow, and explore the meandering and expansive. It's for that reason I'm asking how your love for history developed.

6. The Tale of a Queen Bee and a Double Life

Dear Emilia,

Before telling how I fell in love with the past, I want to linger in the present to discuss how you rid yourself of writer's block. It was a more complex process than simply rediscovering *Twilight*. It required that you work through the disconnect that caused and perpetuated the block. To do that you had to transform the chore of writing the college essay into a means for fulfilling your purpose.

Until you resolved the tension between your desire to be admitted to college and your desire to critique the entire admissions process, you were blocked. *Twilight* was the means to satisfy both ends. On the one hand, it would impress any admissions committee as a serious and unique topic. On the other hand, *Twilight* gave you a context for voicing your reservations about higher education without leveling a self-destructive attack.

In more abstract terms, the block disappeared once you demonstrated agency on your own behalf. Instead of perceiving the college essay as nothing more than an opportunity for packaging yourself, you chose to perceive it as a means for expressing your concerns. By doing so, you transformed this rite of passage into an educative experience. However, to be fair, you didn't do it entirely by yourself. Some credit should be given to your schooling. At sixteen, would you have read Bourne on your own?

As to your question about the origins of my love of history, the short answer—two girls, one boy, and a city. The longer answer is an epic tale of a queen bee and a double life. Sure I learned some history in elementary school -- the standard stories about pilgrims and presidents. And whenever my extended family gathered to celebrate a holiday some uncle would recount the trials and triumphs of relatives who immigrated here. Those conventional encounters with the past piqued my curiosity. My passion for history, like Achilles shield, was forged as a defense. His shield defended him against Trojan spears; my passion protected me against the social humiliation inflicted by eighth grade girls. Later on, exploring the city and leading a double life strengthened my love for the past.

Her name was Helena and we were to be friends for life. Although life in this case spanned just seven years from ages six to thirteen. It's an archetypical female story, a friendship lost due to unsynchronized biological clocks. Helena at thirteen looked like my seventeen-year-old sister, and like her, had a consuming interest in boys. I at thirteen looked pretty much as I did when I was eleven, maybe a little ganglier. As for boys they were white noise as far as I was concerned.

From your own middle school experience you probably remember that budding sexuality, whether in the guise of bras, periods, or sexual exploration, is the dividing line between girls who sit atop the feminine evolutionary ladder and those who haven't managed to get out of the sea and make it to land. In the Darwinian world of junior high girls I ranked among the latter.

This became apparent on the occasion of Helena's thirteenth birthday. Two weeks before the great event I overheard some of her friends discussing the upcoming party. Their chatter prompted me to obsessively check my mailbox for the invitation, but it was consistently empty.

I was in such deep denial about the cooling off of our friendship and Helena's effort to distance herself from me that I had already bought her a gift. It was the book that inspired the movie *Born Free*, one of her favorites. The movie told the true story of Elsa, an orphaned lion cub taken in by Joy and George Adamson, Kenyan game wardens, and eventually returned to the wild. Helena and I saw the film when the intensity of our friendship was at its height. I remember she was so moved by it that on the way home Helena pledged her life to saving wildlife—but that was before she decided to save boys.

29

With only three days before the party I told Helena I hadn't received an invitation and was worried that it was lost in the mail. That was a big mistake. I mentioned the oversight in earshot of her entourage, which consisted of the eighth grade's queen bees and wannabes. Maybe if I had told her one-on-one, Helena's response might not have drawn so much blood, although the odds of that happening weren't good. In actuality I was yesterday's news and had to be discarded.

"No, the mail didn't screw up, I didn't send you an invitation," she said.

"But I already got you a gift, the book *Born Free*," I announced.

As soon as I uttered that sentence I knew Helena's perception of me as being hopelessly clueless was cemented. I stood there stunned, listening to the laughter of her clique, desiring nothing more than to crawl into the nearest locker.

Shocked? Hurt? Angry? Confused? You bet. Compounding the misery was the fact that I was nearly thirteen, which according to my calculus was too old to go crying to Mom and Dad. I got home that afternoon and tried to be as matter of fact about the incident as possible. But eventually my mother got the whole story punctuated by my profuse sobbing. "Well," she said, "it takes courage not to be one of the crowd. If they don't like you for who you are then you don't need them."

Easy for her to say. She didn't have to navigate junior high's treacherous waters where the penalty for not conforming to the rules of budding womanhood is ostracism that makes Napoleon's stay on St. Helena seem like a holiday. But Mom had inadvertently thrown me a lifeline, one that rescued me from sinking into self-pity and provoked my passion for history. It was the word courage. That word triggered an association. My parents owned the memorial edition of President Kennedy's *Profiles in Courage*. Now I had a reason to read it. If courage was what my mother thought I demonstrated throughout this ordeal, then who better to confirm her opinion than the man I idolized? If President Kennedy agreed with her, then maybe the rejection I experienced would prove to be my finest hour.

I have to admit I skipped most of *Profiles in Courage* except for Robert Kennedy's foreword and the last chapter, "The Meaning of Courage." I still own the copy I read back then and this was the passage I underlined. "In whatever arena of life one may meet the challenge of courage, whatever may be the sacrifices he faces if he follows his conscience—the loss of his friends, his fortune, his contentment, even the esteem of his fellow men—each man must decide for himself the course he will follow."

Not that I was aware of it then but those words ignited my desire to study history. They made me feel less lonely. Granted, it's a stretch to equate Edmund Ross's vote to acquit Andrew Johnson as analogous to my facing down a swarm of eighth grade queen bees. But I was not looking for a one-to-one-correspondence. I was looking for role models. I began to study history with the purpose of emulating what was best in the persons I admired.

Fast-forward two years and there I am with Rose and Ian in New York City. They supported my double life, a life in which I played the part of urban explorer. For anyone who knew me at the time, the idea that there was a part of me hidden from view would seem completely out of character. There were no indications that I wasn't who I appeared to be. I still lived with my parents in Bergen County, New Jersey, went to the local high school where I was an A student, had jettisoned my middle school pariah status and had found my social niche within a small circle of friends. All of it, as far as I was concerned was merely a cover. My real life commenced on Saturday at six a.m. when I took the NYC bound bus to accompany Rose to her dance lessons. During the next sixteen hours I could finally do what I wanted. I was free to explore the city and hang out with Rose and Ian, friends whose passions affirmed my own.

First a little background about Rose. I met Rose when I was six. We went to the same elementary school and took ballet lessons together. Whereas I was mainly interested in my tutu

31

and slippers, Rose was serious. By the time she was eight Rose had auditioned and was accepted to the School of American Ballet. By the time we were in high school she had transferred to the Professional Children's School, next door to Lincoln Center. There she was able to take classes at the School of American Ballet and fulfill her graduation requirements. To this day I consider Rose a person who had a formative influence on me. Here was a friend whose discipline, determination, and self-possession reassured me that those qualities were also within my adolescent reach.

Saturday mornings started with a subway ride to Lincoln Center. While Rose took her ballet class, I walked around with no specific agenda other than acquainting myself with the territory that extended as far north as the Metropolitan Museum of Art and as far south as the Forty Second Street Library. It was on one of those meandering walks that I discovered the Gotham Book Mart. Gone now, the Gotham Book Mart was located on Forty-Seventh Street for most of the eighty seven years it existed—from 1920 to 2007. I still remember strolling along Forty Seventh Street and discovering this small, dusty, cramped looking shop staking its claim amidst the bling of the Diamond District. The discreet sign that hung outside its door intrigued me —"wise men fish here." That sign coupled with the shop's no-nonsense window display of poetry books, plays, and novels was all the invitation I needed.

Entering the shop I was immediately surrounded by history. Books old and new claimed every shelf and surface. Posters announcing past art exhibitions and literary events decorated the walls leading to the lecture room above the shop. Among the events that had taken place there were meetings of the James Joyce and Finnegan Wake Societies. Then there were the photographs. The walls were covered with photographs of poets, novelists, playwrights, artists, and actors who had given readings or talks amidst the piles of books.

One photograph in particular grabbed my attention. It was a group shot dated December 1948. The only people I recognized in it were Tennessee Williams and W. H. Auden because

I had seen photographs of them on books required for English class. Curious about the others, I asked the clerk who they were and what occasion brought them together. He explained that the occasion was a birthday party given for Osbert and Edith Sitwell and then he identified the other people in the picture: Elizabeth Bishop, Marianne Moore, Delmore Schwartz, Randall Jarrrell, Steven Spender were the names I remember. He might as well have given me an anthology of twentieth century American poetry and told me to read the table of contents.

I cherished the Gotham Book Mart like I cherished the city. Both were places where the past was present. From a young age I was interested in how things got to be the way they are. Like you, I was interested in finding out the back-stories. But in the suburban town where I went to high school, traces of the past were obliterated in deference to the new and presumably improved. The Gotham Book Mart, like the city that surrounded it, helped to strengthen my resistance against cultural amnesia, an affliction that attacks a person's sense of reality causing it to narrow and atrophy.

Even though New York is known as a city with an ambivalent relation to its past, the city can't completely erase it. History is encoded in its buildings, streets, design, open spaces, and inhabitants. I became serious about history while exploring New York because it prompted me to formulate my own questions about the past. I didn't know it then, but asking my own questions about something I felt passionate about was the first step toward finding my purpose.

I would leave the Gotham Book Mart around twelve to pick up Rose at Lincoln Center, and then we would meet Ian for lunch. Rose had introduced me to Ian. Like Rose, he also had an aspiration—to become a writer. Unlike most adolescents who say they want to write, Ian was training to write like Rose was training to dance. He was a dedicated note taker and a voracious reader. A born and bred New Yorker, Ian mastered the fine art of simultaneously walking the city's streets, dodging traffic, and reading. His appetite for the written word was eclectic—everything from Spiderman comics to Kafka's diaries.

Just as it would be rare to find Ian without a book, the same could be said about his notebook. It was his constant companion. He would fill its pages with snatches of overheard dialogue or character sketches of individuals who caught his eye. Ian's jottings inspired me to cultivate the common book habit. Common books are blank bound books. I used them to record my thoughts about what I read. I also copied excerpts I found especially meaningful or beautifully written. It's a habit I still practice. By copying passages that moved me, I was beginning to pay serious attention to the way sentences were constructed and word choice. Like my love of history, I was beginning to discover that I loved a well-turned phrase and took delight in ideas that wouldn't leave me alone.

One idea that hasn't left me alone is the idea of the city as educator. Last summer I drafted a preliminary syllabus with the intention of turning that idea into a course, which I hope to teach as early as next year. I have attached a copy of its most recent incarnation. Feedback would be most appreciated. Once I finish its reading list, I will present the syllabus to my department. They'll decide if *The City as Educator* is ready to be offered as a senior elective.

My idea for the course came from three sources. The first was my adolescent encounter with the city. In the company of Ian and Rose I learned about Kafka's trials, Balanchine's choreography, where to find the perfect egg cream—information I considered meaningful, but not the information I needed in order to do well on the American history AP. Even though navigating the city with my friends was just as much a means towards achieving my education as my formal schooling, I didn't consider it that way. Like you, I conflated schooling and education, resulting in my discounting the educative power of my own experience. One of the reasons I want to teach this course is to disabuse students of this misconception. Using the city as my topic, I want students to ask themselves what educates, and to recognize that answers to this question aren't confined to the classroom.

The second source for the course proposal was the recognition that many students attending Alden had circumscribed experiences of their city and therefore had only partial and often erroneous perceptions of it. They are in the city but not of it. This became evident several years ago when a student came to me with a question about finding primary sources for his research paper on W. E. B. Du Bois. I suggested that he visit the Schomburg library. The next day he came back with a look on his face that would have made you think I asked him to take a voyage to Mars instead of a subway trip to Harlem. If this was an isolated incident I could dismiss it as the reaction of one cloistered high school student. Unfortunately that didn't prove to be the case. Over the years, I've come to realize that it's more likely for an Alden student to have spent time on a different continent than in a different borough. Another reason I want to teach *The City as Educator* is to make the case for resisting the gated community mentality. I see this course as a means for encouraging students to redraw their personal maps of their city, maps that would include people and locales not securely within their comfort zones.

The third source of the city as educator idea was Raphael's fresco *The School of Athens*. I have always loved this work. In my opinion it depicts an ideal situation, one where the disconnect between schooling and experience doesn't exist. The scene is one of intense activity, with Raphael's figures disputing, measuring, and conjecturing. The young mingle with adults who go about the business of life and serve as their mentors. By observing and speaking to the geometer, the student depicted in *The School of Athens* understands that the geometric proofs he's studying are as much the building materials of his city as the stone and marble he touches.

For me this fresco portrays the possibility of bringing together the roles of student and citizen within the public life of a city. It's a portrait of what a city would look like if it lacked gated communities, whether material or intellectual. What the student knows, the knowledge and skills he has acquired are the tools he uses to leave his stamp on the city. That stamp is the public manifestation of what on a more personal scale is his purpose. *The School of Athens* portrays a place where schooling and experience are not alienated from one another; it's where what a student knows grounds who he aspires to become.

7. Emilia Launches a Campaign to Pop the Bubble at Alden

November 11

Dear Doc,

WOW!!! Have I been blind. This syllabus opens my eyes to views of my city that I haven't really paid much attention to before. It makes me notice all sorts of things in my everyday life—how the change of seasons affects where people walk, who I see coming to school, returning home, doing errands. I'd love to spend a semester really concentrating on it. I bet my classmates would too. WHOA!!! There's an idea!

Your syllabus gave it to me. If it's alright with you I'd like to propose *The City as Educator* to the Curriculum Committee which meets next Thursday, the 17th. I know you want to finish the course's reading list and talk about it with the history department, but I think *The City as Educator* is the solution to the senioritis problem. It should be made available to more students than the sixteen that could sign up for it as an elective. I will propose that all seniors take your course during the second semester. As I understand it, the Committee has to review and to pass any curriculum change that goes beyond the department level. With your permission, I want to launch an all-out campaign to make that happen.

Your course offers seniors a chance to decide what they need to know. An opportunity like that could transform second semester from four months of marking time to four months during which a senior's high school career comes to a meaningful end. I think my classmates will support my campaign. After years of sitting, listening, and reading about other people's interpretations of just about everything, *The City as Educator* gives us the opportunity to get out, to explore the city, and to come up with our own ideas. I think Alden's seniors are more than ready to do some exploring and by that I mean more than hitting the streets to check out different parts of the city. Exploring for me also describes a different way of learning, one that relies on a person's experience to generate questions and to figure out how to respond to them. Isn't that what happened when you were leading your double life with Ian and Rose?

Because the questions you ask in the *City as Educator* are open, they give students a chance to be both students and their own teachers. By the time a student is ready to graduate from Alden she has learned a ton of subject matter and the strategies to manage it. Formulating questions, choosing the appropriate method to answer them, organizing data, evaluating solutions to problems are the study skills we've been practicing ever since lower school. Aren't those the same skills that make for good teaching? My point is, by the time you're a second semester senior you have the skills to be your own teacher.

In an earlier letter you mentioned a person's inner voice. Couldn't you describe it as a dialogue a person has with herself, during which one of the voices can be identified as the student and the other the teacher? If the point of the dialogue is to recognize and achieve one's purpose, then much of it would focus on deciding what to learn, clarifying why you learn it, and figuring out how—just the topics a teacher and a student would discuss. If the purpose of an education is to cultivate that inner voice, then *The City as Educator* would give Alden students a chance to hear their own.

I also want *The City as Educator* to go school-wide because of the reaction to Chris's comment at the last town hall meeting. Who would have thought his comment about finding it easier to talk to students in our sister school in Kenya than to students attending the public school two blocks away would cause so much controversy? I think his comment hit a nerve because it revealed what everyone knows but no one acknowledges—how superficial all the talk about inclusiveness is around here. The truth is it's easier to get to know the students from Kenya who are here as exchange students than it is to talk with the students who attend Alden from the outer boroughs. Some kids thought Chris talked truth to power. But most were either angered by or dismissive of his statement. Some kids even came up to Chris afterward and called him a hypocrite. They accused him of failing to renounce his privileges while doing his best to make sure everyone else felt guilty about theirs.

For all the talk about diversity that goes on at this school, we never talk about what is glaringly apparent, which is Alden's lack of economic diversity. My friends and I call that the bubble. I think Alden does little to challenge the assumptions the bubble generates about privilege and success. While I don't expect *The City as Educator* to cause any senior to give up his privileges, maybe the project will make him less certain about categorizing people who live outside the bubble as losers and not worthy of concern. I know it's a long shot, but I think it's one worth taking.

The attitudes associated with the bubble have been a source of frustration and anger for me during high school. I'm embarrassed to admit it, but it wasn't until ninth grade that I began to realize most of what I take for granted, everything from not worrying about paying for college to eating right, signifies a privileged life. The bubble nurtures and perpetuates this type of cluelessness because the message it incessantly proclaims is, "You have worked long and hard and are entitled to the privileges you have earned." Pariah status awaits anyone who dares question this belief by asking: Worked hard compared to whom? What are the privileges I've actually earned? Did I earn them on my own?

Throughout high school I've become increasingly uneasy about the relation between privilege and success. The first rumblings happened at a sports dinner during my sophomore year. Sitting at the table listening to the coaches, observing the parents who were there to celebrate their kids' athletic achievements, I suddenly realized how much power—financial, business, social, political, philanthropic, artistic—was concentrated in Alden's cafeteria.

Recognizing that, I understood why life is sweet inside the

bubble. It's just so easy to get things done. While everyone on the outside has to spend time and energy figuring out how to get the information they need and then go through a labyrinth of procedures to do so, those on the inside can usually get their questions answered or a favor done by networking with the parents whose kid attends the same school as yours, plays on the same team, acted in the same school play, goes to the same summer camp.

That's when I remembered the bubble's core belief: you are entitled to enjoy your privileges because you've earned them. OK, but looking at the masters of the universe gathered in the cafeteria I asked myself, what have I and my friends done to earn the access to power we have? If a successful person is someone who proves herself worthy of joining those already inside the bubble, then what's left to prove if you're lucky enough to be born an insider?

Like Chris I'm not going to renounce my privileges. Will giving up what I have help anyone else? The source of my unease is not guilt but doubt. I've come to doubt whether I have an accurate sense of my own capabilities. The bubble can give a person a bloated idea of her accomplishments and her power to influence her circumstances. The question I worry about is whether the power I think I have is real or merely an appearance.

The college process only added to my doubts. It made me face the unnerving possibility that the meritocracy is rigged. Just like some banks are too big to fail, my classmates and I are too privileged to fail. Everything is done to make the transition from high school to college smooth, personal, and successful: meetings with the college counselor in groups, one-on-one, and with the family, summer trips to scout out colleges, prep courses, application coaches, contacting a family friend who just happens to be an active alumni connected with the school at the top of your list, all are standard operating procedures inside the bubble. So what if it's not for people living outside? It's not as if anyone is stopping them from doing the same.

The problem is I don't believe that. You see I also live a

double life. I am one of those Alden kids who is an inside-outsider. I consider myself in the bubble but not of it. I know people's first impression of me is that I'm totally in. Why would they think otherwise? I walk, talk, look, and most of the time act like an insider. Where I go to school, where I live, and the economic security I enjoy support that impression.

But I'm an insider with an asterisk beside her name like a baseball player whose record breaking stats are suspect. My parents—one is a children's book illustrator the other is an architect—have built a secure and comfortable life for my sister and me. That being said, I don't feel deprived knowing that skiing down Vail's slopes or snorkeling around St. Barth aren't options for my Christmas break unless I pay for it. At my twenty-first birthday party I won't be disappointed when among the presents there's no trust fund with my name on it.

One of the advantages of being on the bubble's periphery is that you maintain friendships with outsiders. I hang out with kids who go to public schools throughout the city. I get to hear what they're dealing with, go to places beyond the bubble's approved zip codes, and find myself constantly questioning the assumptions I hear at Alden about the people on the outside. At the same time I have to contend with outsiders' assumptions about people on the inside: I try to convince them not everyone with a trust fund is the enemy. I'm committed to *The City as Educator* because I'm committed to bursting bubbles, breaking barriers and trespassing boundaries that turn neighbors into losers and enemies.

Enough of my reasons for making *The City as Educator* my mission. I am ready to go before the Curriculum Committee and argue for it becoming the senior class's culminating project. I'll propose that your course go school wide because it fulfills two functions no other course currently does: it allows students to own what they study and to step outside the bubble. I anticipate that the Committee will want to know how a course originally developed as a history elective for sixteen students can be transformed into a project for one hundred. I've attached the plan I've devised so far.

Let me know if you have any objections to me going before the Committee and making the case for *The City as Educator* as the senior project. Are you all right with the change in focus from the city to its neighborhoods? All that means is that the questions on your syllabus would pertain to a neighborhood each group explores rather than the city as a whole. The only stipulation is that the neighborhoods cannot be the ones that are included in the bubble—no Upper West or East Sides, Park Slope, Soho, Battery Park City.

By the way, the Curriculum Committee's meetings are open to all students and teachers although no one ever comes. If you want to show up on the 17th, that would be great. Otherwise the minutes are always posted. Finally, may I show the syllabus to some of my friends and get their reactions to the plan?

8.   Doc Lays the Groundwork for a Teachable Moment

November 12

Dear Emilia,

Shocked and awed is probably not too grandiose a description of how the Curriculum Committee will react to your plan. You were eight and probably too young to remember when President Bush and his advisors assumed Iraq could be shocked and awed into becoming the Middle East's city on the hill. The blowback proved them wrong. I mention this because I think you should be prepared for unexpected and possibly negative reactions from the Committee. At the very least, don't lose sight of something you already know: change occurs slowly at Alden. The Committee might decide your plan is too destabilizing to support, owing to the time pressure they'll be under to pass it for this academic year.

That being said, I have no objection to you presenting your plan. Towards that end I have sent an email to the Chair and cc'd it to the members. In the email I included a copy of the syllabus, explained my reason for giving it to you, and assured them that you have my permission to use it as the blueprint for the senior project. I also informed them that if your plan is rejected I would follow my original intention and present *The City as Educator* to my department with the goal of offering it as a senior elective for next year. One word of advice, I urge you to e-mail your plan to the Chair. He and the other members will need time to read it before the meeting.

Through experience, I have found that the fastest way to alienate members of any bureaucratic committee is to surprise them with documentation on the day of the meeting. By not providing the Committee with the information it needs beforehand, you put its members at a disadvantage. Feeling ignorant and flustered at the start of the meeting, they'll be less receptive to what follows, no matter how well you argue your case.

I decided to write the email rather than attend the meeting on the 17th. Adopting *The City as Educator as* the senior year's culminating project is your vision and you'll be its most forceful advocate. The minutes will provide me with the official account of what happened and then I expect to hear your analysis. As for your friends, I have no objection if you want to discuss the syllabus with them. I would ask them for their opinion about *The City as Educator* as the senior project and as a history elective. I suspect they will have two different reactions. When faced with the possibility of real change, you might discover your peers are more supportive of the status quo than you anticipated.

Learning that you lead a double life as an outside-insider, gave me some insight into your commitment to *The City as Educator* and your ambivalence about Alden. One advantage of living on the bubble's periphery is that it offers an excellent vantage point from which to critique it. In no small part, your plan's emphasis on exploring diverse neighborhoods and creating the blog are means to achieve that end. The vision you have for *The City as Educator* might make it easier for Alden students, who don't live in the bubble's designated zip codes, to discuss the disconnect they often experience between school and their neighborhoods without singling out that cohort as a curiosity. If your plan accomplishes that it will have accomplished much.

At this point, I think you are more than ready to make your case before the Committee. But you know as well as I do, even if your presentation on the seventeenth is flawless, there are circumstances affecting the Committee's reaction that are out of your control. It's a situation that leaves a person feeling uneasy and resigned, not unlike the emotions associated with finishing and mailing off a college application.

One way I've found to maintain some semblance of equanimity when you have a lot on the line and limited influence is to figure out if there's an outcome you desire that doesn't depend on another's will. In your case, is there something in your plan that will not be affected by the Curriculum Committee's decision? I think there is. It's the other way of learning you mentioned as one of the reasons for implementing your plan, what you called exploring.

All those characteristics you ascribe to exploring—the student deciding what she wants to know, the student as teacher, the student relying on experience to generate questions and responses to them—I ascribe to study. Rest assured, study has long predated the Curriculum Committee and whatever the outcome on the seventeenth, it will continue to exist. Given that, it seems like an opportune time to examine study.

Contrary to conventional wisdom, a school isn't designed to be a place for study. Everything about a school—its structuring of space, its organization of time, the roles its constituencies fill is dedicated to instruction. Unless a school adopts some unique policy, study isn't a priority.

"Nonsense," is how a proponent of conventional wisdom would respond to my assertion. "That is an absurd statement. Haven't you ever said I'm studying X when you're talking about school assignments?" "Yes," I would reply, "but that's not what I am actually doing. To be precise I'm learning X." "Well what about study hall, or is there something wrong with that term too?" "Quite frankly there is. It should be renamed learning hall."

By now my imaginary interlocutor, exasperated by what he interprets as pedantic usage battles, would be searching for the nearest exit. What he perceives as useless hairsplitting over the meaning attached to learning and studying, I interpret as another example of conflation—just as misleading as the one between education and schooling. As a culture we conflate learning and studying because we conflate study and instruction. Both studying and learning, like study and instruction, are necessary if a person is to form herself, to discover her purpose, to achieve her education. For that reason it is important to be clear about the differences between these ways of knowing.

Learning is the action of receiving instruction to acquire

knowledge. A pupil learns what is imparted to him. That's what occurs in schools. The origin of what he learns comes from an outside source; that source is usually a teacher teaching a course. Studying is the action of applying one's mind to acquire knowledge whether by books, observation, or experiment. The origin of what a student chooses to study emerges from within; that source is her inner voice. That occurs in living her life.

Describing study as a lifelong process begs a question: How do you find a place for an activity that is characteristic of being alive? You could build an addition to your house and designate it the study. That might work, assuming you have a house and the money for the renovations. But there's a drawback to this approach. Having to meet those conditions, study is relegated to a privilege of the few instead of a human possibility claimed by all. How about this? Since a person needs a place to study throughout her life, that place needs to be easy to rearrange in order to accommodate changes that occur in her lived circumstances. It also has to be highly mobile. The only place I can think of which fulfills those criteria is a person's inner life.

Assuming that a person's inner life is study's address then how is it furnished? Not all that differently than its brick and mortar counterpart. Both contain furnishings that function to ignite and affirm a person's desire to seek out what matters. Walk through most built studies and you will find books, works of art, instruments—scientific and musical—mementos of all sorts, photographs of significant people and places. All serve as signposts and tools for the owner's quest to create meaning in her life. Because the place for study located in a person's inner life needs to be mobile and easily reconfigured, the signposts and tools she depends on to create meaning are dematerialized. Instead of tangible objects you have experience, questions, images, and ideas. Taken together these are the elements of an education. From them the on-going dialogue a person has with herself emerges.

What does a person have to do to make these elements

hers? This is another way of asking about a point you raised in an earlier letter: What does a person have to do to own her education? The answer is the one you formulated. A person explores; a person studies. Doing so she brings a mindful attentiveness to her experiences, regardless of whether those experiences are mundane or marvelous. Her alertness, call it her readiness of mind, serves as study's energy source. This heightened sense of awareness fuels a person's capacity to wonder. The wonder she feels awakens her desire to give it significant form. To study, to explore is to search for the symbols that will enable a person to transform her feeling of wonder into a language that makes it intelligible to herself and eventually to others. That is the work of the inner life and the poetry of the inner voice.

Wonder isn't instruction's strong suit. Instruction's strength is imparting information with the goal of doing so efficiently and effectively. That becomes apparent when you stop to consider the label we give to instruction's content—the course. Can you think of anything less amenable to exploring than taking a course? How do you explore something that's completely laid out even before you engage it? Most of the time it's impossible.

But teachers worthy of the title have a desire to do the impossible. They create courses peppered with back roads, detours, even a sense of the wild in the hope that their instruction will generate wonder in a student resulting in her transforming what she learns into what she studies. *The City as Educator* is my attempt to do that.

To be honest, on one level *The City as Educator* is a failure. Through it I wanted to recreate my adolescent experience of the city, when in the company of Rose and Ian I made the city my place for study. No course can do that because no course can replicate a person's experience and sense of wonder. At best, by making the city a subject for study *The City as Educator* might inflame a student's desire to make it a place for study. The difference between something being a subject for study and a place for study is profound. It goes to the heart of the difference between schooling and achieving an education. As a subject for study the city like most subjects learned in school has little effect on who we are or how we choose to live. The city as subject rarely penetrates one's inner life. But as a place for study the city becomes a cultural feast of symbols, signs, languages, images, sounds, textures and tastes that beckon a student to sample and digest. Ever alert to affinities that resonate between one's inner life and the city, a person discovers clues, catches intimations of who she might become and how she might live. That was the gift the city gave me. *The City as Educator* is my attempt to acknowledge it.

I came across this excerpt the other day and copied it in my common book. I think it is a wonderful description of a city functioning as a place for study. Clive James wrote, "In the late nineteenth and early twentieth centuries, Vienna was the best possible evidence that the most accommodating and fruitful ground for the life of the mind can be something more broad than a university campus. More broad, and in many ways more fun. In Vienna there were no exams to pass, learning was a voluntary passion, and wit was a form of currency. Reading about old Vienna now, you are taken back to a time that should come again: a time when education was a lifelong process. You didn't complete your education and then start your career. Your education *was* your career, and it was never completed."

For Raphael it was ancient Athens, for Clive James it was early twentieth century Vienna, cities that were places for study in a world of instruction. Whatever the Curriculum Committee decides about the fate of the senior project, the more significant decisions to be made are yours. Will you make the city your educator? Will you make twenty-first century NYC your place for study?

9. Blind-Sided by Good Intentions

November 18

Dear Doc,

What a fiasco! And the worst part of it is I should have seen it coming. There were signs even before the Committee met that the plan was going to go nowhere. Several days before the meeting I circulated the syllabus among friends. As a history elective they liked it, but as the senior project not so much. Chris's reaction was the least negative. He was convinced the Curriculum Committee wouldn't pass the plan because it disrupted business as usual at Alden. As he saw it, the administration and faculty would continue to talk about reforming second semester, but as long as seniors maintained their grades, were admitted to college, and graduated—little would change.

Lilly simply thought I had lost my mind. She made it clear that having worked her butt off for thirteen years, second semester senior year is her time to kick back. The last thing she wanted to do, and she kept reiterating that she wasn't alone in her opinion, was to take on a project that required her to schlep all over the city. Lilly reminded me that she, like every other Alden senior, was determined to keep second semester free of outside commitments. In her opinion it's what the class deserved considering the marathon of keeping up with classwork, completing applications, and preparing for the SATs that filled up the fall. Lilly also made it clear that the topic she and many of our classmates least wanted to explore was NYC. She wanted to know why I didn't realize that most kids chose the colleges they did to escape the craziness of urban life.

I was disturbed by Chris and Lilly's reactions, but it was Luis's criticisms that undermined my confidence in the project. I met Luis two years ago when he became an intern at my Dad's firm. The firm has an outreach program for public school students who are interested in architecture. A perfect day for Luis involves having the time to walk the city, looking at buildings, identifying their styles, noting when and by whom they were built.

Last Christmas, I gave him the *AIA Guide to New York City*. No matter how miserable the weather he and I would go building watching. Like your friend Ian, Luis also keeps a notebook. In it he records his reactions to buildings. Luis calls it his source book and according to him it serves two functions. First, it provides ideas for structures Luis believes he'll eventually design. Second, Luis takes it with him on college interviews to demonstrate his passion for architecture.

My friendship with Luis was in the forefront of my mind when I devised the plan for the senior project. Luis lives in the Morrisania section of the Bronx. Even though I'm a native New Yorker it was only after meeting him that I set foot in that borough. In a way, Luis is my ticket out of the bubble. With him I explore parts of the city I would never visit on my own. Most importantly as friends we trust one another. Luis comes to my apartment and I visit him at his. We know each other's families and friends. As friends we talk about the differences in our lives and why they exist. The senior project was my attempt to recreate my experience with Luis on a school wide basis.

That is not how Luis saw it. The plan made him angry. He compared Alden students visiting neighborhoods not in their comfort zone to anthropologists studying the natives in some remote African village. He assured me that the blog and "forcing" a relationship between Alden and high schools throughout the city would never work. Most of his friends, Luis pointed out, dismiss Alden kids as so different that they see no reason to have anything to do with them. When I reminded him about our friendship, Luis said that was different. Our friendship, he explained, grew out of a real situation—his internship at my Dad's firm and not some bogus school experiment.

By the time the 17th arrived I had lost confidence in the plan. Listening to the Chairman's opening remarks I knew it was a dead issue. His first few sentences were about the work I put into formulating the senior project, what a visionary take on second semester it was, and how it will enlarge the range of subsequent discussions about the topic. I knew the plan was dead because instead of discussing it, the Chairman was complimenting me for doing it, a tactic I recognize as building someone up in order to let them down as gently as possible.

After I gave my presentation, I was commended for the boldness of my vision but told it would be impossible to implement the plan by January. It raised questions that would take time to answer. The Committee focused on two: Would teachers who teach senior electives during the spring semester give them up to become the project's facilitators? Is the school legally liable for students' welfare when they are working on a school assignment not during school hours and off site? All told the actual discussion of the plan took ten minutes. The other fifty were devoted to study.

I should say independent study. The Chairman latched on to the part of my proposal about exploring, and used it to start talking about the school's independent study policy already in place for second semester. The good news, as far as he was concerned, was that its popularity keeps growing but its success has created a problem: the workload was not equitably shared across the departments. History and English got many more independent study requests from students than math and science. The rest of the meeting was spent determining how to solve the problem. By this time I zoned out and was relieved the meeting was ending, as was my campaign for *The City as Educator*.

I failed. At least I think I did. The only interesting part of the meeting was at the very end. The Chair said that although my plan was too ambitious to be implemented in such a short amount of time, the Committee was grateful for my insights about Alden's independent study policy. News to me! I never brought up that policy. It seems, "students deciding what they need to know," is the one phrase the Chair and the Committee heard me say. By the time the meeting was over it had become the rallying cry for getting more math and science teachers to sponsor independent study projects.

It took till the next morning for me to realize that I was the beneficiary of an artful spin job. Sure the plan was a failure, but by the end of the meeting I had succeeded in calling attention to the need for broadening Alden's independent study program. I felt like the kid who is one of the team's worst players but nevertheless comes home with a trophy for most improved. The take away—I failed but I didn't. I began to think about the meaning of success inside the bubble. What does success mean if failure is negotiable? How does Luis's experiences of success and failure differ from mine?

I would like to think my plan failed because it would have made too many people uncomfortable. By making my classmates explore neighborhoods outside of their comfort zone and interact with students of different backgrounds, I hoped to enlighten them, to make them realize how much the system is rigged in their favor and to question whether they're entitled to the privileges they enjoy. But I think it's more likely the plan failed for the same reason you considered *The City as Educator* a failure. Like you, I tried to turn the lessons I learned from my friendship with Luis into lessons everyone should learn. But it doesn't work. If one of my classmates tried to do the same to me, turn a personal experience into a lesson, I'd be the first to bolt. I did just what Bourne warned against: I got so caught up in how to bring the project off that my means ruined the purposes I wanted to achieve.

At this point, I'm tired and disappointed, but not ready to give up on the city as educator as a possibility for myself. I've been thinking about taking a gap year and volunteering for the City Year program. Whether or not I do, I still have to get accepted to college. Thanks for writing the recommendations for me. I know those are a lot of work. So the one piece of good news is I'll send out my college applications after Thanksgiving break. At least for the immediate future, there's no campaign to launch, no college admissions deadlines to meet, and maybe I'll get some sleep.

10. Cultivating the Fine Art of Detachment

Dear Emilia,

Yes, I think Bourne would be chagrined at the plan you devised but wouldn't write you off because of it. For what it's worth, you aren't the first person who didn't see it coming. Few people can deploy the necessary detachment that makes it possible to critically judge a project they are passionate about. Along with not seeing it coming you also didn't see how ironic your plan was. In trying to make Alden a place for study you created an instructional scenario that rivals a military invasion in its complexity and rigidity.

Completely lacking in the plan were those qualities—serendipity, surprise, meandering, discovery, even getting lost—that make studying a city pleasurable. Walter Benjamin, one of the twentieth century's most astute observers and appreciators of urban life wrote, "Not to find one's way around a city does not mean much. But to lose one's way in a city, as one loses oneself in a forest, requires some schooling." The schooling Benjamin had in mind is the capability to immerse oneself in the presence of a city. Unfortunately, that spirit was lost amidst your project's logistics.

I kept silent about all of this because I thought it more important for you to discover a fundamental lesson about changing institutional practices of long standing: a disjunction can easily develop between what you intend to do and how you do it. In other words, don't assume that because your ends are noble, that alone justifies the means you choose to implement them.

So what if your plan had more in common with Mao's Cultural Revolution than the Buddha's search for Enlightenment? I don't think your campaign was an unmitigated fiasco. You sell yourself short if you think the good that came out of it was

53

just spin. The plan failed, but does that mean the city as a place for study is a dead issue? Even though Alden's seniors aren't going to occupy the outer boroughs, is involving the science and math departments in the school's independent study program a defeat? At the very least you were able to test the limits of innovation at Alden and get a more accurate reading about what's possible.

Things fell apart because in your enthusiasm for *The City as Educator* you allowed your passion to override your judgment. Don't get me wrong. Passion is not a failing—quite the contrary. Being passionate about something or someone is a condition that humanizes us. It warms the spirit, fuels the imagination, and ignites a person's desire to bring something new into the world. But living at the peak of passionate intensity isn't a steady state. At some point a person has to ask herself the tough question: how can I sustain what I care about?

That's where the art of detachment comes in and at seventeen years old you are only starting to serve your apprenticeship. So cut yourself some slack. Not only are you a beginner, but also the art of detachment is extremely difficult to master. It requires a person to examine the motives and meanings she assigns to her actions from a vantage point outside of herself. An unsettling state of mind and one most people do their utmost to avoid. It's as if that inner voice we've been discussing splits and simultaneously acts as both defense and prosecuting attorney. One voice defends the soundness of the judgments a person makes while the other challenges them.

But you're learning detachment and are fortunate in your teachers. Among the best people to instruct you are Alden's coaches. Like strength, speed, agility, and endurance, detachment is an attribute that an athlete needs to cultivate. Unless varsity sports have changed radically since I played field hockey in high school, I imagine coaches still give a post-game wrap-up during which they analyze what went well, what mistakes were made, and what the team needs to do to improve. I have heard Coach Griffiths call that "the good, the bad, and the ugly speech," and as a longstanding member of the soccer team you have probably heard multiple versions of it.

Coach Griffith's instruction in the art of detachment is subtle. By focusing on the team, he provides his individual players with an alternate perspective, one that broadens their visual field. Seeing the larger picture, each team member evaluates her performance in the context of the team instead of fixating on what she alone accomplished on the field. In effect playing a team sport teaches a person to detach herself from her own self-absorption.

Like all instruction, learning the art of detachment has its scope and sequence. As a beginner you are provided with an alternate vantage point from which to critique your actions. A team, a family, a school, a company, a religious organization are all examples of ready-made perspectives that take a person outside of herself. As you get used to the practice of looking at yourself from an objective viewpoint, the next and more advanced lesson is to internalize it. Instead of depending on something out there, like a team, to provide you with an alternate perspective, you create it yourself by internalizing a set of standards. Formulating standards and using them to make objective judgments about what you do is the work of the inner life.

Actually you have already learned this advanced lesson about detachment regarding your writing. Think back to the first history essay you wrote for me and to your reaction to the C- I gave it. Upset about getting a grade lower than a B+, you came to see me, ready to defend its worth. Like most ninth graders, you started the discussion talking about yourself, how many hours you spent writing the essay and how hard you worked. It took a while, but eventually I got you to leave yourself out of the discussion and to concentrate on ways to better organize the words you'd written. Clearly, as a ninth grader you hadn't yet learned to detach yourself from your work and to critique it. One of the big differences between Emilia then and Emilia now is that you have internalized the standards for good writing and become your severest critic.

Yet even as seniors, a significant number of students lose

their sense of detachment when faced with its most demanding test—the college admissions process. They can't perceive the process as something distinct from themselves, as an institutional decision about the mix of persons that will best represent college x's vision for its incoming freshman class. Instead these seniors live on the razor's edge, regarding an acceptance or a rejection as a judgment about their personal worth.

Like all powerful arts, a person has to use the art of detachment discerningly. If it becomes the default relationship she has with herself, a person loses the sense of herself as a whole; she loses her sense of integrity. The feel of that condition is painful and at times dangerous. A person spends her life going through the motions because she's detached from what she does. It's what you call clearing the hurdles. At the extreme, a person can become so self-alienated that she thinks of herself as an object, living her life without a purpose of her own choosing.

That is why I say, "let it go," about not seeing what's coming, and move on. Your passion for *The City as Educator* was misguided, but nothing to berate yourself over. In fact, I hope there will be many more occasions during your lifetime when you find yourself swept away, head over heels, totally there, in the zone, or as Emerson put it, "a mind on fire." Those experiences, ripe with fulfillment, are the best protection we have against sleep walking through our lives and settling for whatever.

PS I almost forgot. The department received a memo concerning senior requests for independent study. You need to write a formal statement describing the topic, why it interests you, and a preliminary reading list. Later we can set up meeting times and decide the approach to take. I need to have the request before we go on Christmas break.

11. Emilia is Definitely Not in a Holiday Mood

December 11

Dear Doc,

If females can lose their mojo, mine has disappeared into a witness protection program. By the time I read your letter I was beginning to surface from my campaign funk, but then life got in the way in the form of the Senior Breakfast, early decision acceptances, and Luis. Each pulled me back into the doldrums. As for detachment, right now I'm joined at the hip to disappointment, envy, and hurt.

Listening to returning seniors speak about their first three months of college life was disappointing. Although I knew it was a long shot, I nevertheless wanted someone on the panel to describe how exciting they found their courses. Instead there was talk about whether to go Greek, advice on how to handle the roommate from hell, examples of campus diversity, urgings to study aboard, accounts detailing the variety of extracurricular activities college have to offer—athletic, service oriented, political, social, entrepreneurial, and artistic. After listening to all of this, the only question I had for the members of the panel was how they found time to go to class.

The truth is my friends who are first year college students aren't brimming over with excitement about their classes or academia in general. Basically they describe their course work as not all that different from what they experienced at Alden. Sure, as college students they are assigned more to read and it's covered at a quicker pace. But on the bright side, there're fewer written evaluations and no one gets bent out of shape if you don't make it to class.

Afterwards I talked to Nick Kantor. He said the quality of teaching was better at Alden than college. As far as he could tell, teaching was a distraction for academics. From the TA's who conducted his discussion sections, to the junior faculty who taught most of his classes, the impression he got was that teaching and especially teaching freshmen was time lost from the more important business of writing papers that would convince colleagues that you were tenure worthy. I had heard this before, but I'd be lying if I didn't admit I wish it were different.

For me the highlight of the Breakfast was the Q and A session. Tiffany asked the members of the panel if there was something they wished they had learned in high school that would have made the transition to college easier. Their answer was almost unanimous—budgeting time. But it was budgeting time with a twist. The difficulty these returning seniors faced wasn't the usual challenge of making a to do list and then scheduling time to get everything done, what I call the hurdle version of time management. Everyone on the panel agreed that when a student graduates from Alden that kind of budgeting is practically encoded in her DNA. What they found difficult was deciding what to do with their free time. Do I study? Party? Chill? Leave campus?

I can relate. For Alden students most days are so crammed with activity that having to make choices about how to spend free time isn't an issue. Apparently college changes that because of its more open and flexible schedule. One panel member admitted to wasting an inordinate amount of free time. Another indiscriminately filled it with activities because he didn't want to be bored, but he ended up bored anyway. A third saw free time as an opportunity to ". . . add to and diversify her resume." "Times are tough," she informed us. "You need to start building a resume as soon as possible. One that will demonstrate to a prospective employer why he should hire you and not the other well qualified applicants." Sounds like the college sweepstakes all over again. Except now the grand prize is a well-paying first job that will launch your career. As I see it, wasting free time, filling it with activities simply to fend off boredom, or using free time to pump up your resume are the effects caused by thirteen years of hurdle clearing.

The disappointment I felt listening to these returning seniors was largely gone by the time we got back from Thanksgiving break. But then colleges started mailing out their early decision letters. When friends told me they were accepted I was surprised by my reaction. Outwardly I congratulated them, but inwardly I was one big ball of envy. At that moment, kids I had known for most of my life were nothing more than the competition. Even at the brunch held to celebrate Lilly's acceptance to Harvard, I was busy calculating what her acceptance might mean for my chances in April. Not only did I envy Lilly for getting into Harvard, I envied everyone else accepted early. For them the college process was officially over—no more deadlines, recommendations, interviews, and waiting. For me there was four more months.

The one sentence that kept running through my mind was, "It should have been me accepted early to Harvard. It should have been me taking my place among this year's college sweepstakes winners." Even though I thought I had managed to remain detached, I was surprised at how much I had bought into the process. Right now, if my life was a graphic novel there would be a panel where I would be telling Lilly how happy I am for her and how much she deserves to go to Harvard. But the bubble over my head would simply say, "Yeah right! I deserve it more." I hate this Dr. Jekyll Mr. Hyde existence. It makes me feel terrible and it makes no sense. I was the one who decided not to apply early, so why hold Lilly's acceptance against her? As you say, it's time to move on. It's probably the only way to get out of my schizoid head.

But moving on isn't going to be easy because I might have wrecked my friendship with Luis. While the Breakfast was disappointing, and the early decision episode brought out the worst in me, the tension between Luis and me hurts. He's still angry over my plan for *The City as Educator*. For some reason just the thought of kids from Alden exploring neighborhoods like his has made Luis mistrust me. I'll admit my plan was insensitive maybe even ignorant, but as I explained to him it was never intended to hurt anyone. And it never happened: no one went anywhere.

None of this lessened the tension between us. The last time I spoke to Luis he said he wondered if I thought of him, his family, and his neighborhood as a community service project. That did it. I lashed out, asking him if the only reason he pretended to be my friend was to get in good with my father so he could get a summer internship. One thing you can say about friends, get them angry and they can rip each other to shreds.

Before this mess happened, Luis and I were planning to spend most of Christmas vacation together. One of the books I've been reading is Patti Smith's *Just Kids*. I had this idea about visiting all the places in the City that made it a place for study for Smith. I started to make a list of them with their addresses. The point was to see how many still existed, which ones had disappeared, and what had taken their place. Luis liked the idea because many of the places that Smith wrote about are near Cooper Union. If Cornell doesn't take him, Luis hopes Cooper Union will. The walk would have given him a chance to check out its neighborhood. The other day I screwed up my courage and left a message on Luis's cell phone. I said we should talk and asked if he still wanted to do our Patti walk. So far, no reply.

The upset with Luis has made me feel stuck. I regret what I said and constantly think about it. That makes it difficult to move on. So I haven't come up with an independent study topic. At first I thought of doing *The City as Educator* on my own. I'd pick a neighborhood and explore it. But the idea of doing it alone doesn't do much for me. Then I thought about reading more essays by Bourne. But having written about him for my college essay, I need some time away. However, the last line of *Twilight of Idols*, where he mentioned William James, has made me curious.

The only fact I know about William James is that he was the brother of Henry. What I'd like to find out is why Bourne wrote, ". . . I evoked the spirit of William James, with its gay passion for ideas, and its freedom of speculation, when I felt that slightly pedestrian gait into which the war had brought pragmatism." Why did Bourne single out James for such praise? Between now and Tuesday I plan to do some basic research about him. By Thursday you'll have my topic proposal.

12. To Move On,
Emilia Is Advised to Let Go

Dear Emilia,

From what you've told me about Luis I suspect he is having the same regrets you are about the blow-up. The next move is his. Until he makes it you are faced with the difficult task of patiently waiting. Even though your first reaction might be to dive in and settle this misunderstanding, Luis needs time to sort out his feelings. If you intervene before he is ready, I fear the intrusion will only widen the rift between the two of you.

Like you, my initial response to a problem is to solve it as quickly as possible. That way I feel I'm in control and can prevent events from becoming more chaotic. Patience for me, and I think the same holds true for you, is a virtue that goes against type. It calls for a letting go, which I find unnerving. To wait patiently is to admit there are forces I can't control because they haven't had time to make themselves known.

With Luis, you don't know the reasons why a plan that never got off the ground has caused him to mistrust you. It's possible he doesn't know either. Since so much is ambiguous the best course of action is to wait patiently, to step back and allow what is not apparent to surface. Otherwise by acting prematurely you risk amplifying the problem you originally sought to solve.

Think of the term, patient, or better yet, think of your sophomore year. As much as you wanted to get back in the game, your torn ligament had its own timetable. It didn't matter that the team was poised to win the championship; you had to wait patiently allowing the healing process—a process of invisible, incremental, and complex steps—to do its work. If you had returned earlier to the playing field you would have jeopardized and prolonged your recovery.

Experience had taught me that often the best course of action is to wait patiently. If patience is not easy for me to practice it is particularly difficult for someone as young as yourself. At fifty-seven a person going through a rough patch has been there many times before, knows this too will pass, and understands that sometimes the wisest action a person can take is to let it be.

At seventeen a rough patch can look endless because the present eclipses the past and the future. When the present becomes all a person can envision, she is apt to believe that the way circumstances are currently arranged will last forever. She becomes trapped in the eternal now. To free herself from this truncated version of reality she needs to cultivate patience. It provides time for events to run their course and circumstances to change. What's at stake is more than getting through a tough time. Without the ability to be patient, the thought that what is will always be becomes the source for both panic and despair.

Resilience along with patience is the other virtue that sustains a person going through tough times. Neither you nor I can predict whether Luis will call. If, over time, it becomes apparent that he won't, then you'll need to draw on your reserves of resilience to move on from the hurt. Unlike patience, a virtue not usually associated with someone your age, resilience is considered the hallmark of youth. To be young, fit, and privileged is to embody resiliency. But that's a misconception based on a sentimental and unrealistic interpretation of youth that casts it as a time of life untouched by suffering.

The erroneous belief that resilience is youth's birthright and will simply manifest itself when needed is particularly strong when it comes to kids born into privilege. Sure, the resources they command go a far way to shield them from many, if not all, of life's frustrations and heartbreaks. But even the privileged, with all their safety nets at the ready, can't transcend the human condition. Inevitably they will have to grapple with the randomness of ill fortune in the guise of loss, despair, sickness, and loneliness.

In fact being born into privilege can easily weaken a person's resilience. Having depended on others to smooth over reality's rough edges, accustomed to garnering overwhelming praise for underwhelming effort, a person born and bred inside the bubble has no need to exercise her capacity to bounce back. I'm not recommending suffering or deprivation as character builders, but at some point even the most cosseted person will face rough times. Whether she has it within herself to move on is not a *fait accompli* but as open a question for the privileged as it is for the rest of us.

Why are some people more resilient than others? How is it that a person whose life can only be described as one trial after another, nevertheless manages to keep her perspective and humanity intact? While another person born with every advantage crumbles. I don't know, but I can speculate. Whether a person is resilient or not, I think depends on her ability to cultivate a sense of fulfillment. In fact I would argue that resilience is rooted in fulfillment.

This seems straight forward enough, but once again we are dealing with the problem of conflation. As with education and schooling, or learning and study, people usually conflate fulfillment with success. Contrary to what most people believe, success and fulfillment are not synonymous. A person can be successful without being fulfilled or fulfilled without being successful. The fundamental difference between them is the point of origin for each. Success is a condition generated by externals—external standards, procedures, and rewards. Fulfillment emerges from a person's inner life as she makes choices, prosaic and transformational, that shape her. Fulfillment is the consequence of a person's search for meaning in her life, for her purpose. Resilience is grounded in that search.

The forms resilience takes are as individual as the persons who deploy it. In Woody Allen's film *Manhattan* the character Allen plays, Isaac Davis, is lying on a couch distraught at the turn his life has taken. To keep himself from wallowing in despair, he begins to recite reasons why life is still worth living. Isaac creates an *ordo amoris*, an ordering of what he loves based on his lived experience.

Whether the items on the list have contributed to his success doesn't matter. What does matter is the films, the music, the persons, even the foods that have infused Isaac's life with meaning and provided him with a sense of fulfillment. Reciting his list to himself, Isaac activates his sense of resiliency. The connection between fulfillment and resilience is made apparent in the next scene. Isaac moves off the couch, seeks out the person he loves, and gets back in the game. The movie ends before we know if Isaac is successful, whether he and Tracy have resumed their relationship after a six-month separation. What we do know is Isaac is at least resilient enough to hope they will.

I think students go off to college expecting they will find it automatically fulfilling. When that turns out not to be the case they find numerous reasons, as exemplified by Nick's comment on the quality of college teaching, to become disappointed, if not cynical. As sound as their critique might be, many undergraduates rarely consider what they bring to college. What are the questions, interests, and purposes that have meaning for them? Most know how to amass the credentials that will facilitate their climb up the ladder of success, but few ask themselves why make the climb. So is it any surprise that college becomes another four years of hurdle clearing and far from fulfilling?

But it doesn't have to be. The one big difference between four years of college and the seventeen that preceded it is the possibility of leisure, what the returning seniors call free time. Judging from how the panel members used leisure, they operated under a misguided notion of what it is. At least they're not alone. Their confusion is shared by multitudes.

Leisure, a word culturally overworked and imprecisely understood, shares those distinctions with words like education, study, and fulfillment. Ask several people to define leisure and the chances are they will mention free time followed by a description of how they like to spend it: watching a game, going out to dinner, seeing a movie, surfing, taking a nap, reading something enjoyable. The one trait these seemingly disparate examples of leisure have in common is that they aren't associated with work. Putting the pieces together we can define leisure as time cordoned off from work's demands and reserved for those activities a person finds relaxing, entertaining, enjoyable, exciting, and/or restorative. There's nothing surprising about that except it's the antithesis of leisure's original meaning. This makes it worth our while to investigate the difference between leisure's past and present definitions.

Go to the OED on line. Look up leisure, click on etymologies and scroll down to the eighteenth and nineteenth entries. You should come across the words scholastic and school. Click to get their full entries. Surprised? The ancient Greek word for leisure, σχολη, is the origin for the Latin *scola*, German *Schule*, and English school. That's right, long ago and in civilizations not that far away leisure was defined as the work done in pursuit of an education. But what kind of work was that? Simply put, to study something whole, to study something for its own sake, to study it because you find doing so intrinsically fulfilling.

Sounds like no big deal, but studying something whole is a radical act. While doing it, a person temporarily reconfigures the categories, cultural and/or private, which usually shape her understanding. It's the turn of mind that can disrupt the relentless pace and single-minded focus demanded by clearing the hurdles. Much of what we learn in school—contrasting, quantifying, comparing, distinguishing, abstracting, deducing, proving—are ways of knowing that enable us to sustain a single minded focus. Success in clearing the hurdles is achieved by persons who don't allow their gaze to stray from their goals.

Ways of knowing that concentrate a person's attention on a single goal aren't renounced when she is studying something whole. Rather, they take a back seat to contemplation, appreciation, comprehension, and wonder. Each of these has the power to distract a person clearing the hurdles because they reorient her focus. It's not that a person experiencing this distracted state rejects the categories that make up what we commonly call reality. It's simply that in this state the categories don't matter because she has relinquished the desire to control reality for the possibility of comprehending it.

The liberation from worn constructions of reality leaves a person simultaneously lost and aware, buoyed by the sense that it all could be another way. She begins to question whether the focus of her attention is worth the effort and if the course laid out to achieve her goal is one she wants to run. Instead of interpreting the world through the linear logic of the next step, the motion associated with hurdle clearing, she meanders—seeking connections between herself and what she studies.

The desire to study the whole can be ignited by a person, a question, an idea, an image, an experience, even an object. It is the desire to know rooted in what a person loves and finds fulfilling. That knowledge affirms her trust in herself to explore beyond the actual, to seek out her purposes. Why is studying something whole, which entails giving oneself over to something regardless of whether the outcome will be successful, fundamental to finding fulfillment? Without ever experiencing what it is to study something whole a person lives her life captive to what is, unaware that it might all be some other way. In other words she lives without a sense of possibility and is sentenced to live at the beck and call of the actual's contingencies. Since those contingencies are constantly being manipulated by others more powerful than she, she lives her life as their tool, renouncing any chance of fulfillment.

To study something whole is to take a stand affirming the desire to cultivate one's sense of possibility—one's inner life. Letting go of the usual categories that define and delimit experience, a person is forced to attend to the voice inside—maybe hearing it for the first time amidst the cultural glut of sensory overload and mind numbing cant. Hearing that voice is essential for discovering how one should live.

All of this speculation has its practical side. Second semester is looming and even though you missed the early decision boat, you too will have more free time. Instead of fixating on whether Luis will call, something beyond your control, or berating yourself for feeling jealous about Lilly's early acceptance, which only proves you aren't this year's candidate for sainthood, use your leisure, your independent study, to grapple with something whole. I look forward to finding out what that will be.

13. Emilia Stands Her Ground

Dear Doc,

A day after I read your last letter, my Dad had a talk with me about Luis. He suspected something wasn't right because of the way Luis was acting at the studio. Instead of being his usual outgoing and focused self, Luis was uncharacteristically withdrawn and distracted. At dinner, Dad asked if I knew what was troubling my friend. I told him about the fight.

Forget patience. Dad advised me to clear the air as soon as possible. He suggested that I make a surprise visit to the studio and talk with Luis face-to-face. I said I'm not ready to do that. I told him, I've tried to contact Luis by phone, and as far as I'm concerned the next move is his. We left it at that, but I could tell my Father wasn't pleased.

Then I got your letter. I don't have the patience to wait for Luis to decide whether he's my friend or not. So I've come up with a plan; actually it's my new year's resolution. If Luis doesn't call by the start of the year, I'll go to the studio and confront him.

For now, I'm finishing the independent study proposal. It will be on your desk by Friday morning.

INDEPENDENT STUDY PROPOSAL
WILLIAM JAMES

Submitted by Emilia Carlyle

December 16

I am proposing to read and write about several of William James's works for my independent study project. I became interested in James while drafting my college application essay about Randolph Bourne's "Twilight of Idols" (1917). In that essay, Bourne criticized his fellow intellectuals, foremost among them John Dewey, for supporting America's participation in World War I.

Bourne started "Twilight of Idols" with two questions addressed to James:

"If William James were alive would he be accepting the war-situation so easily and complacently?"

"Would he be chiding the over-stimulated intelligence of peace-loving idealists, and excommunicating from the ranks of liberal progress the pitiful remnant of those who struggle 'above the battle'?"[1]

And then Bourne ended the essay with an explanation of his reason for "evoking" the spirit of William James as an ally against Dewey's position on the War—"Malcontentedness may be the beginning of promise. That is why I evoked the spirit of William James, with its gay passion for ideas, and its freedom of speculation, when I felt the slightly pedestrian gait into which the war had brought pragmatism."[2]

Reading "Twilight of Idols," I became aware that for Bourne something had gone wrong with pragmatism as Dewey and his followers interpreted it. Assuming this to be the case, I would like to find out what James meant by pragma-

---

1   Randolph Bourne. *The History of a Literary Radical and Other Papers*. (New York: S. A. Russell, 1956), p. 241.
2   *Ibid.*, p. 259.

tism and whether he would have joined Bourne in opposing America's war effort in 1917.

I am also interested in James for more personal reasons. I looked him up in Wikipedia and under the section labeled careers, the first paragraph lists all the positions he held at Harvard. I was struck by the fact that James basically grew up and grew old at that one institution. Forty-three years is a long time to spend anywhere, given that in today's world we are told to expect to spend no more than ten years of a career at one place. I find it remarkable that James entered Harvard as a medical student in 1864 and retired as emeritus professor of philosophy in 1907. Reading him, I hope to discover how today's Harvard differs and resembles the university he knew and what James's view on education was.

With my questions about pragmatism, Harvard, and education, I propose reading the following for my independent study:

Pragmatism (1907)
"The Ph.D. Octopus" (1903)
"The Social Value of the College Bred" (1907)
"Talks to Students on Some Life's Ideals" (1898)

14. Learning to Love
the Questions Themselves

December 16

Dear Emilia,

Although I haven't had time to focus on it, I looked at your proposal and think William James would make a terrific independent study topic. I look forward to reading him with you. In my opinion, offering independent study as a course option for second semester seniors is the best innovation the Curriculum Committee has instituted since I began teaching at Alden. For both teachers and students it's a game changer. Ironically that might be why so few take advantage of it. The possibility of switching instructional roles, the student becoming the teacher and the teacher becoming the student, many find disconcerting. Although touted as a fine idea, I suspect when it comes to actually doing an independent study, many teachers and students perceive it as too much work for the student and too much control for the teacher to relinquish.

Well, I'm not among them. In fact I might be independent study's most ardent fan. It is the one time, during thirteen plus years of instruction, when a student has the opportunity to study something whole. She becomes both teacher and student and I find the melding of those roles revealing. I'm always surprised at how much more demanding students are of themselves when they take an active role in creating their own course of study. The first list of readings they submit for my approval usually contains more than any human being could possibly finish in a semester. Your preliminary list is no exception.

Then there are the questions. They are the aspect of independent study that intrigues me the most. For many students it's the first time they're responsible for formulating them, and that has a destabilizing effect. By putting the responsibility for forming questions on the student instead of the teacher, the obsession with getting the correct answer, a basic goal of instruction is subverted.

Independent study is not for the intellectually timid. It demands an adventurous spirit because it invites teachers and students to entertain the radical notion that the end of an education is to continually query the given, regardless of whether an answer exists, let alone a correct one. Independent study is a powerful game changer because it presents the student with a possibility that contradicts the reality she's embraced throughout her schooling. That the sum of the correct answers she's collected over the years doesn't form her, rather it's the questions she asks that do.

Usually during the first meeting I have with my independent study student, I hear why he or she developed an interest in a particular topic. The topics I have sponsored have been the communist revolution in Cuba, female soldiers fighting in the Civil War, Plato's *Republic,* and fascist imagery. As varied as these topics are, the consistent delight I get from sponsoring an independent study can be traced to one source. I'm thrilled to witness a student falling in love with the questions themselves.

Last but not least, the best to you and your family for the New Year.

15. The Year Ends with a Rapprochement and a Walk

December 30

Dear Doc,

GREAT NEWS! Luis called. We must have talked for over an hour. We went on about how sorry each of us was for what was said. We also agreed to talk things out in the future, before they have time to fester and threaten our friendship. Taking him at his word, I told Luis I still had some unfinished business about the fight. It's the point you brought up in a previous letter. I asked Luis why *The City as Educator* caused him to mistrust me. And why his mistrust didn't disappear when it became evident the project was dead in the water.

His reply was honest and disturbing. In fact I'm still thinking about it. According to Luis, he had a choice to make. Either he could see me as a rich, white, privileged girl or as Emilia Carlyle. Luis explained that *The City as Educator* brought that decision to a head. Although he never mentioned it to me, Luis was getting flak about our friendship ever since I first visited his neighborhood. That was almost two years ago. Most of his friends thought of me as the enemy, or as they put it, the vanilla latte princess. I was the person who invaded their turf and whitened up their friend. By the time of our fight, Luis's friends had made it clear that the only way he could demonstrate his loyalty and street credibility was to dump the princess.

All of this was news to me. Not because I'm oblivious about the tensions that set New Yorkers against each other, but because whenever I visited Luis I felt welcomed by his family and the handful of friends I met. I now know Luis carefully chose which friends I'd meet. They were either kids attending the City's special high schools or kids who got scholarships to private schools.

Isn't there a saying about the wisdom of hindsight being

20/20? Thinking back over the two years since we've been friends I should have realized that my presence in Luis's neighborhood was making him uncomfortable. Over time, his invitations to visit the Bronx were becoming less frequent. Luis seemed more at ease when we met at my father's studio and hung out in Manhattan.

While I was waging my *City as Educator* campaign Luis's friends were escalating the pressure on him to end our friendship. They blamed me for his desire to go to a college far away from the neighborhood. They also believed that as soon as I got what I wanted from him, though that something was never made clear, I'd dump him. For Luis, *The City as Educator* project appeared to confirm his friends' suspicions. All of a sudden my plot was revealed. The vanilla latte princess was going to use him and his whole damn neighborhood for a school project that did nothing except make her look good.

As Luis explained, the reason he took so long to call was that he needed time to sort out how he felt about all of this. Should he go along with his friends' perception of who I am or should he go with what he knows, that Emilia Carlyle is a person he can trust. Luis's inner voice proved stronger than all of his friends' and he decided to see me as a person and not as a category.

As I was listening to Luis's explanation I tried to remain calm. I didn't want him to become the target of my rage. Although calm and controlled on the outside, my inner voice was screaming for blood. "What idiots his friends are. Yeah they got two out of three right. I'm a girl and I'm white. Rich? They don't have a clue what rich is. I'm taking Luis away from the neighborhood? What are they, stupid and blind? Why would anyone stay if they could escape?" This internal drama would have continued if Luis hadn't reminded me of something I'd said. "Em, remember when you were pissed off at some of your classmates because of their sense of entitlement? You said they believe they're too privileged to fail. Well you're that person to my friends. To them you are too rich to fail while they struggle not to be too poor to succeed."

Luis's comment hit home. When I realized his friends see me as I see the most arrogant inhabitant of the bubble, a person who believes she is entitled to her privileges simply because she exists, my rage started to dissipate. It was the insight that allowed me to practice detachment. As my rage subsided, I thought about success, failure, and what it meant for Luis and me. Even though I locate myself on the bubble's periphery, Luis and his friends see me embedded in it. In their view that means I have second, third, even fourth chances to make good. Luis and his friends operate on the principle that they don't. They know that they live without the safety nets I take for granted, and for the most part, they have to create the conditions for their success in a way I never will.

Take a simple matter like homework. When it becomes a topic at Alden, it is usually because students are complaining about the amount they have. In my thirteen years at the school, I've never heard any of my classmates voice a concern about finding a place to do it. For Luis that's a major worry. He depends on his neighborhood public library for the quiet to concentrate and for a computer to use. Often both are in short supply because of the large numbers of people for whom the library is their primary source of information and community.

Then there are the days he can't get to the library. Luis's father is out of the picture and his mother is the family's sole financial support. Occasionally she's stays late at work and then Luis has to pick up his younger brother and sister at their after school programs and begin getting dinner ready. Although this doesn't happen often, when it does Luis can't use the afternoon and early evening to do his own work or intern at my Dad's firm.

Although hardly ever talked about at Alden, money is always a concern for my friends outside the bubble. The colleges they will attend are as much a matter of which one gives them the most financial aid as it is about their abilities or preferences. Hanging out with Luis, I'm constantly reminded of what a huge role necessity plays in the lives of most people and the impact it has on their chances for success. Luis has to spend an inordinate amount of time and energy finding the people and programs to help him overcome the obstacles that necessity puts in his way.

Because his school doesn't offer free SAT prep classes, Luis had to locate a place where he can get help. He commutes to the Kingsbridge Heights Community Center to get the tutoring he needs. In my case I simply dropped by Ms. Albin's office, asked what tutoring program she would recommend, walked there, paid the fee, and started preparing. Wasn't it Woody Allen who said that 80% of success is showing up? Watching Luis, I've learned it takes a lot more energy and time to show up at the right place at the right time when you live outside the bubble.

For Luis, necessity can easily morph from a series of hurdles to a series of roadblocks. Owing to a lack of information, resources, and support, he often experiences the challenges necessity presents as either/or situations, which have the potential to shut down his options. For those of us protected by the bubble, necessity rarely closes off options. Instead it becomes a series of negotiations. When pressed, insiders deploy their wealth, contacts, and power to prevent a hurdle from becoming a brick wall. Unlike Luis we can command the information and the coaching to make sure the hurdles necessity throws our way will not prevent us from achieving what we desire.

The whole college admissions process illuminated these differences. In no small part my rant was against the portion of the Alden community that is comfortable with the fact that necessity can undermine a person's dreams for no other reason than who his parents happen to be. It bothers me to imagine that the bubble's true believers think that as long as Luis has the right to apply to Cornell's architecture school, justice has been served. In their minds the only reason he wouldn't make it is that the hurdles were just too high and he lacked what it takes to clear them.

I call those individuals true believers because they cultivate a willful blindness in order to believe they are entitled to the privileges they enjoy. Their blindness leads them to conclude that since there are no laws that prohibit a person from improving his lot in life, success is a possibility for all. According to their worldview, if a kid like Luis doesn't become an architect, he has only himself to blame. "Sure, it's tough out there," they'll concede, but since nothing is blocking Luis from going after his dream, it's only his lack of determination, smarts and character that prevent him from achieving his goals. One day spent among Luis and his family quickly trashes that belief.

When it comes to considering the life chances of a person like Luis, true believers expect him to tame necessity largely on his own. That way he proves he has the right stuff. That strikes me as bogus. When it comes to themselves, true believers say they have made it on their own, but in reality there are entourages of counselors, tutors, nannies, advisers, coaches, doctors, learning specialists, teachers, mentors, references, stylists, consultants, family, and friends ready and able to assist.

Their self-imposed blindness allows true believers to go to bed at night assured that the system society uses to identify its winners, mediocrities, and losers is a just one. If, on the outside chance injustices emerge, true believers have that contingency covered. They set up foundations and bankroll philanthropies as a means of righting the wrong and are able to sleep the sleep of the just. Ask any true believer how she became a success. It's always due to extraordinary feats of individual effort. Anyone who questions whether she has actually earned the privileges she enjoys or suggests that those privileges result from undue entitlement is dismissed as envious of her excellence.

What I've learned from all of this is that Luis and I didn't fight about *The City as Educator*. Like Luis said it was just the tipping point. Having gained a little perspective on what happened, I realize the fight had its origins in my friend's frustration. Luis has had to spend his life walking a tightrope between two untenable attitudes. On one side the true believers proclaim Luis has only himself to blame if he doesn't succeed. On the other side his friends make sure Luis understands that if he tries to succeed he's a sellout. I wish I knew what would make those attitudes disappear. Maybe then Luis wouldn't have to waste his energy balancing on a tight rope. Instead he could come down to earth and concentrate on what my classmates and I take for granted—figuring out how we want to live.

At least when Luis and I hit the streets and went on our Patti walk he returned to earth. Both of us were amazed at how much this city has changed since 1967. What was depressing was how many of Smith's significant places have disappeared or, like Scribner's, have lost their identity. Smith knew it as a bookstore and publishing company. Now it's part of a cosmetics franchise. As Luis and I were looking for traces of Smith's and Mapplethorpe's city we realized that in addition to being just kids in the late sixties, they were just lucky to live in the city at that time. They were lucky because they could find jobs and cheap places to live making it possible for them to survive on little while pursuing their art. Over sandwiches at Katz's, Luis and I wondered if the conditions that enabled Smith and Mapplethorpe to go after their dreams can still be found anywhere in our city.

Here's to the New Year and getting to know Henry's older brother.

16. Investigating the Octopus that Threatened Harvard

January 11

Dear Doc,

I know second semester doesn't officially start until the beginning of February and you haven't yet approved my reading list, but I wanted to find out about "The Ph.D. Octopus." I love the image! I found it on Emory's website about William James, along with a list of his other works. From the amount he published it seems writing for James was as natural as breathing is for everyone else.

"The Ph.D. Octopus" (1903) was the right choice to start off my independent study. I enjoyed it. Last year when I was writing my history research paper, I read several secondary sources written by professors. Let's just say I slogged my way through them. Even though eminent historians wrote the books, I found their prose lifeless. Reading James, I hear his voice and it keeps me interested in the issues he raises.

Along with giving a voice to his argument, James sets the scene for it as his brother sets the scenes for his characters. I wonder if William and Henry read and critiqued each other's work. Anyway, James starts "The Ph.D. Octopus" with a concrete story instead of a set of abstract definitions, disembodied facts, and mind numbing statistics. The story James relates is about a "brilliant student of philosophy" who he knew when the student attended Harvard's Graduate School, and who was denied an appointment to teach English literature at a "sister-institution." The reason the student was denied the appointment was that he left grad school before completing the Ph.D. process. It wasn't that he was incapable of doing the work, it's just that the student saw no reason to get a Ph.D. in philosophy when the position he was applying for was to teach English literature. Unfortunately for the student, the college he thought would hire him didn't see it that way. He was given a year to get his doctorate or else the teaching position would be offered to someone else.

In the ensuing months the student wrote a brilliant and original philosophic thesis instead of spending his time preparing his literature courses. As brilliant and original as the thesis was, Harvard's Ph.D. Committee, of which James was a member, couldn't pass it. According to James the work didn't pass because, "Brilliancy and originality by themselves won't save a thesis for the doctorate: it must also exhibit a heavy technical apparatus of learning: and this our candidate had neglected to bring to bear. So, telling him that he was temporarily rejected, we advised him to pad out the thesis properly, and return with it next year, at the same time informing his new President that this signified nothing as to his merits, that he was of ultra Ph.D. quality, and one of the strongest men with whom we had ever had to deal."

Only after the members of his thesis committee sent separate letters testifying to the student's excellence did the College agree to allow him to ". . . retain his appointment provisionally, on condition that one year later at the farthest his miserably naked name should be prolonged by the sacred appendage the lack of which had given so much trouble to all concerned."

So what's James criticizing in this essay? The obvious answer is the credentialing mania, which he warns is beginning to spread its tentacles over academia. O.K., but how does this mania specifically deform higher education according to James? Here's the part where I almost fell off my chair. The toxin James's Ph.D. Octopus spews out over academia is the relentless often thoughtless categorizing of people.

For James the octopus that threatened Harvard symbolized the havoc that's unleashed whenever powerful and reputedly intelligent people become so obsessed with credentials that they fixate on a category to the exclusion of attending to the person they are assigning it to. James observed the effects of categorizing just as it was emerging as an issue. A little over a century later I think it has become so common that people hardly notice it anymore, except if they feel the category they're assigned is unjust. Like the time Luis's friends labeled me the vanilla latte princess.

Be assured Doc, my ears are ringing. I can hear the warning you repeatedly gave my class about misreading a historical document. "A historian must resist reading the past as merely a reflection of or a lead up to the present." Those words had a big impact on me. For the first time I realized there's more to doing history than acing the test. You made the point that as historians each of us is responsible for marshaling evidence that would convince a disinterested reader that our assertions about the past are credible. Well, I think I can do that by explicating several passages from the essay.

Take this one for example. "To our surprise we [the thesis committee] were given to understand in reply [from the College] that the quality *per se* of the man signified nothing in this connection [securing the teaching job], and the three magical letters were the thing seriously required." As I interpret it, the College President and the trustees' inability to see the student's intellectual life as part of his lived life makes the student's story one of categorizing run amuck. By reducing the student's qualifications for teaching English literature to one criterion, whether or not he has a Ph.D., the President and the trustees blinded themselves to other abilities the student might bring to the position. They also increased the likelihood that the best person wouldn't be hired for the job, making it more likely the College's Ph.D. obsession would serve as a fig leaf for mediocrity rather than an incubator for excellence.

James said as much when he wrote, "The latter, [advanced degrees] therefore, carry a vague sense of preciousness and honor, and have a particularly 'up-to-date' appearance, and it is no wonder if smaller institutions, unable to attract professors already eminent, and forced usually to recruit their faculties from the relatively young, should hope to compensate for the obscurity of the names of their officers of instruction by the abundance of decorative titles by which those names are followed on the pages of the catalogues where they appear."

James finished the paragraph by describing the power

wielded by credentials to beguile. "The dazzled reader of the list, the parent or student, says to himself, "this must be a terribly distinguished crowd—their titles shine like the stars in the firmament, Ph.D.'s. S.D.'s and Litt.D.'s bespangle the page as if they were sprinkled over it from a pepper caster." The last line did it for me. What an image—Ph.D.'s spilling out like pepper from a shaker. As far as I'm concerned, the entire quote is a stylistic triumph. It's written with the wit and commonsense that makes me want to continue reading James.

I suspect he was deeply disturbed by the credentialing madness because he understood, probably before most of his colleagues, that if gone unchecked the pursuit of credentials would undermine the mission of the university, which according to him was to serve ". . . as the jealous custodians of personal and spiritual spontaneity." Thinking back to the Senior Breakfast, all I can say to Professor James is good luck with that. Spontaneity of any sort did not seem to characterize any of the panel's first taste of college life.

So Doc, I'm curious. My first reaction to James's interpretation of the university's mission was to dismiss it as a beautiful but a dead ideal. Today, the idea that a university should serve as the custodian of personal and spiritual spontaneity seems like something Zonker, the perpetually zoned out Doonesbury character, would campaign for during his undergraduate days back in the sixties.

But something keeps gnawing at me. William James isn't Zonker Harris. James's intimate and long-term relationship with Harvard makes it impossible for me not to take his vision seriously. So why does that vision strike me as bizarre? Did it ever flourish? If so when and where? Why and when did the university renounce its role as custodian of personal and spiritual spontaneity and take on its current one—certifier of the successful?

Even more baffling, why did most of James's contemporaries perceive the changes happening to the university as progress? James noted their support for the transformations taking place when he observed, "Schools, Colleges, and Universities, appear enthusiastic over the entire system, just as it stands, and unanimously applaud all its developments." What system was he referring to in 1903? Why did his colleagues' support it? Did James see a connection between their support and the unleashing of the octopus?

How's that for loving the questions themselves?

PS I decided not to apply to City Year. That's at least one letter of recommendation you won't have to write. If you remember I was thinking about taking a gap year, back in November, right after *The City as Educator* project imploded. Life was bleak then and continued that way through most of December. There was the depressing Senior Breakfast, the fight with Luis, my ever-shrinking social network, and long stretches of restlessness and boredom. Truth was I was more turned off by the thought of going to college than committed to becoming a City Year volunteer.

Now, I'm actually excited about the next four years. I think that was the case all along, but in November I mistook a passing mood for a more permanent condition. My parents call it the drama queen part of me. But when I'm down, it's especially difficult for me not to believe that whatever is wrong isn't going to last forever. Maybe it was reconnecting with Luis, jumping the gun on the independent study, relaxing over the break, or all three—whatever it was, I'm over the funk.

17. Doc Recommends Thinking Like a Historian

January 13

Dear Emilia,

From all appearances you've hit the ground running. Take it from me, James is someone you could spend years studying and still not exhaust the riches of his protean intellect. Medical doctor, psychologist, philosopher, critic, professor—the man demonstrated an unbounded curiosity about life that illuminates his writing.

Keep in mind, as you're studying James, that your past was his present and as riddled for him with uncertainty as the present is for you. Try to resist thinking about the man and his ideas as though they were the outcome of a simple chain of events, the trajectory of which was apparent from the start.

Imagine instead, James making judgments about the issues of his day aware that contingencies he hasn't anticipated could easily raise questions about the soundness of his judgments. What I'm suggesting is to give him the same room for deliberation about error that you give yourself when coming to a decision. You, at the start of the twenty-first century, like James during the late nineteenth, make judgments cognizant of your ignorance and doubt. Whether a person is studying the past or deciding how to get through the next several hours of her day that experience, judging in the face of the unknown, is at the core of the human condition.

Most people assume James attended Harvard College, but in fact he entered a different part of Harvard University, the Lawrence Scientific School in 1861. James applied to the Lawrence School instead of the College because his father, Henry Senior, proclaimed colleges ". . . hot beds of corruption, where it [is] impossible to learn anything." My source for these facts is a first rate biography entitled, *William James: In the Maelstrom of American Modernism* by Robert D. Richardson. I asked the

85

school librarian to get a copy and she said it would be on the shelf by the end of next week. I'd recommend you read it to find out how young William was schooled.

In order to piece together the context for some of the reading you'll be doing let me mention a name and a detour that might prove fruitful. Charles W. Eliot played a significant role in James's life. Only eight years older than James, Eliot and James shared a long-term professional association. Their first encounter was in an undergraduate classroom: Eliot was James's very young chemistry professor. Then in 1869 Eliot became Harvard's president, a position he held until 1909. From start to finish, Eliot's presidency paralleled James's career. It's more than likely that the changes in higher education James is reacting to in "The Ph.D. Octopus" have something to do with Eliot's policies.

When it comes to figuring out why categorizing became an issue for James I'd suggest making another detour and revisit a document we discussed in class last year: Lincoln's *Address at the Wisconsin State Fair, 1859*. When you read it this time, think about who's listening to him. Pay close attention to the message Lincoln is sending about the link between free labor, progress, practical experience and formal schooling. Look up the founding date for the University of Wisconsin. Then contemplate what connection might exist between that date, Lincoln's audience, his message, and the problem that categorizing was supposed to solve. Who had much to gain from categorizing and why? What were the tools used to bring it about? What type of society derives its legitimacy from categorizing and the credentialing process that's associated with it? What changes in character would such a social organization evoke? What was James's reaction to this transformation?

Have fun connecting the dots.

18. The World Turned Upside Down and Inside Out

Dear Doc,

I wanted to talk with you after the Memorial Service, but I was too upset. I sat with Lilly and Chris in the back of the chapel. After the service we didn't hang around. The three of us went to a nearby Starbucks just to feel normal again.

It didn't work. I haven't felt normal since I heard about Caleb's suicide. Of the three of us I knew him the best, although I wouldn't say we were close. Our relationship, if you can call it that, was based largely on where we lived. Caleb lived on the Lower East Side. He and I had a running joke about representing Alden's fringe population. We divided the school's students into the citizens—Upper East and West Siders, the fringe elements,—anyone living south of sixtieth or north of ninety-six street, and the immigrants—kids who commuted to school from the boroughs and New Jersey.

In middle school I frequently took the subway home with Caleb. Then he would talk about his love of graphic novels, comics, and movies. In high school, our subway rides became less frequent. Caleb had usually left school by the time I was finished with soccer practice or doing whatever needed to be done on the newspaper. But I remember two times—one when we were sophomores—and the other, last year, when we reconnected.

For some reason I didn't have practice or any other after school commitment. Caleb spotted me and asked if I wanted to go to the Barnes and Noble near school because he needed to buy a book. The book he bought was titled *A Doonesbury Retrospective*. We spent the next several hours in the Barnes and Noble cafe looking at it. Caleb explained Doonesbury's history, who the original characters were, which ones came later, and what their issues were. That's when I learned about Zonker

Harris.

We also talked about what we wanted to do in the future. I said something lame about wanting to write. Caleb was more focused. He said it was a choice between becoming a cartoonist, a graphic novelist, or a filmmaker. We even joked about my writing a graphic novel and he illustrating it. I invited him over to my house so he could meet my mother. I figured as a children's book illustrator she could give Caleb some advice about his plans, but nothing ever came of that.

The other time was last year right after you had given out the list of possible history research projects. During the few times we did manage to go home together, one topic we always talked about was how his section of your course differed from mine. That day he was as excited as the day he bought the Doonesbury book. He was thrilled that among the possible project topics was a section devoted to film. He asked me whether I thought "Birth of a Nation," "Modern Times," or "Invasion of the Body Snatchers," would make a better paper. I said I didn't know because I never saw any of them. Caleb thought that was terrible and offered to teach me about film. He suggested going to the Film Forum. I said I'd get back to him, but never did.

The last, I can't believe I'm writing last, time I had a real conversation with Caleb was after the fiasco with the Curriculum Committee. We had lunch together and he said that he had heard about the project from Chris and thought it was a good idea. I said well, that brings the total of its supporters to three: Chris, himself, and me. He said what I needed was a Marx Brothers film, but I said I had to work on my college essay and maybe we could get together over Christmas break. Nothing ever came of that either.

Now Caleb's dead. I knew he was shy and at times sad, but I assumed all he needed was to graduate from high school and find a place where he could do his artwork full time. I never imagined that the pain he was suffering was so overwhelming that his only way out was to kill himself. I keep going over our conversations and wondering, if I had paid more attention could I've prevented him from committing suicide? I always thought of Caleb as a sweet, gentle, slightly weird kid. I never thought, until now, how desperate he was and how little I did to help him.

19. Attending to the "Fall of Icarus"

Dear Emilia,

I'm going to say something that's vitally important for you to hear: your not paying "enough" attention to Caleb didn't cause him to take his life. To think otherwise is a gross distortion of reality and therefore dangerous. It imbues you with the power of life and death, while reducing the complex human being Caleb was to a set of simplistic responses to external forces. If the root of his despair could be neatly traced to a person and/or incident outside of himself, then maybe I'm to blame. What about all those C's he received from me? Or the times I didn't make an effort to draw him out in class? Or when I was too preoccupied with some bureaucratic deadline to strike up a casual conversation with him? Why wouldn't my acts of inattention be just as likely to have contributed to the hopelessness that destroyed him as yours might have?

Do you recall in one of our earlier letters I talked about adolescents living a double life? Often there's a disjuncture between the self they present for public consumption and their inner lives. In Caleb's case that disjuncture was not only between his public and private selves but it fractured and corroded his inner life as well. When we discussed the inner life, it was as a force for growth and self-formation. For Caleb, I suspect it became a tormentor—constantly reminding him of how inadequate he was. Why his inner voice became his enemy you and I will never know. The tragedy is Caleb didn't either and thought only by killing himself would he be able to silence it.

You might have heard adolescence referred to as the time in a person's life when she loses her innocence. It's considered a necessary step towards adulthood. For the most part the meaning attributed to that phrase is of a young person becoming sexually aware. But that's only a partial interpretation of what a loss of innocence means. Death is the other and less recognized fact of life a young person needs to confront in order to attain her majority. Usually the confrontation is expected —an elderly and ailing grandparent dies. Even in those cases there is regret, sadness, loss and grief. But there is also a measure of solace for those who mourn. They can take comfort in knowing that the life that is no more had time to shape itself. The horror of Caleb's death is he denied himself the right to exist and therefore died unformed. His passing leaves his mourners frantically trying to make sense of what is incomprehensible.

Your letter concerned me. It's almost inevitable to believe that if you had paid more attention to Caleb, or were a little less self-involved, he would still be alive. But you can't be all knowing ahead of time. How can a person tell what to pay attention to before the fact? Even when she has decided what to attend to, how can she discern what is enough attention? In other words how could you have judged that treating Caleb with everyday friendliness was insufficient and to advert a crisis you would have to change your behavior towards him?

To help illustrate the point I'm trying to make, I'd like you to take a look at Pieter Brueghel's painting, "Fall of Icarus," 1590-95. Do you remember the myth? To escape imprisonment Daedalus, Icarus's father, made a pair of wings for each of them. Exhilarated to be free and flying, Icarus didn't pay attention to his father's warning. He flew too close to the sun, which melted the wax on his wings, plummeted into the water, and drowned.

Google Pieter Brueghel's "Fall of Icarus" and you'll get images of the painting. Without being told beforehand it's difficult to see Icarus. His legs are sticking up out of the water in the lower right hand corner. As he careens into the sea the three other figures in the painting also don't see him. The plowman, the angler, and the shepherd are engaged in their work and oblivious to the disaster that's occurring nearby. In this case art imitates life. Isn't it as difficult for us to know where and when calamity will strike as it is for Breughel's figures?

I think that's the reality that this painting illuminates. Because we are mortal, we humans live every second of our lives in death's presence. But instead of fixating on that truth we arrange our lives so we don't have to attend to it. We adhere to our routines and cultivate habits as if we'll go on forever. When death inevitably asserts its claim, its appearance isn't the occasion to ask if it could have been prevented—how can you control what's uncontrollable? Rather it's the occasion that reminds us just how fragile and extraordinary an ordinary day is.

That understanding was made palpable for me the day after 9/11. School was cancelled on the twelfth and like everyone else in the city I found myself at loose ends. Just as you needed to go somewhere to feel normal after attending Caleb's memorial, I decided to walk to Zabar's to buy a loaf of my family's favorite bread. It wasn't the bread I needed so much as the reassurance that the eruption of death that had stunned my city was not stronger than the routines that sustain it.

I remember the walk: it was silent. Not the gentle silence that engulfs New York during a snowstorm, but an ominous hush rooted in fear. When I got to Zabar's, I was relieved to see a few other people there. But my sense of normalcy was short-lived. Making my way towards the bread counter I saw that the shelves were bare. The city was cordoned off: no deliveries were made that morning.

By that time, I had repeatedly seen what would become the disaster's iconic images: the planes hitting the towers, people jumping to their deaths, first responders wading through wreckage. But for me it was Zabar's empty shelves that revealed how vulnerable cities and their inhabitants are. Both depend on complex networks to survive. For the most part those networks hold because they're the focus of someone's attention. Millions of people attend to life's details making an ordinary day possible and extraordinary.

Later in the day my husband and I took a walk along Riverside Drive. The city had cranked up the volume since my morning excursion. Kids and their parents had ventured out and reclaimed playgrounds all along the Drive. Maybe you were busy climbing and swinging at a playground near Hudson Street on that afternoon. As we made our way home, facing northward towards the George Washington Bridge, I spotted them—the huge tractor-trailer trucks making their way into Manhattan. I smiled, probably for the first time in two days. Shelves would be restocked, school would resume, and people would, once again, attend to the demands of living. I think it's time for you to do the same. Lincoln and James are waiting and there's a reading list to discuss.

20. Emilia Follows Her Nose

Dear Doc,

What have I gotten myself into? Geez, I thought I'd read a few of James's essays, maybe a secondary source or two, write an analysis of what I read, and that's that. Instead I'm doing extreme history. No back of the book answers, sources up the whazoo, and hydra like questions: answer one and two more pop up. I miss instruction's nicely bounded history lessons and assignments. At least when it came to classroom history I didn't have to think about where to begin, how to proceed, and what I wanted to find. I always knew what came next. This independent study makes me feel like I'm bumbling around in a labyrinth, exerting a lot of effort but getting nowhere.

That inner voice we've been discussing is saying to me, "O.K. girl, let's face it—you're panicking. After shooting your mouth off about instruction's inadequacies, you finally get the opportunity to study something whole and you want out. Read Doc's letter again. Start with something easy and familiar. Easy would be finding the date the University of Wisconsin was founded. Familiar would be reviewing the Lincoln essay. See if you can uncover any connection between the two. You can do this!"

So it began, Doc. I never expected to react so strongly to study. Who knew it's as much an emotional experience as an intellectual one? My inner voice had to go into coach mode in order to build up my confidence. I needed to believe that if I followed my nose I'd find my way.

First mission: to find the founding date for the University of Wisconsin. No worries. Just google University of Wisconsin, click on Wikipedia, and come up with 1848. Since Wisconsin was one of the schools I considered applying to but didn't, curiosity got the best of me and I went to its official website—

nothing surprising there. Just the usual information geared towards prospective applicants—admissions procedures, academics, student life, opportunities for studying abroad and research. Although the history of the University wasn't featured, I did a search and hit gold. I found a timeline that confirmed Wisconsin's founding date. I also found the digital version of a four-volume history that covers the years from 1848-1971. First lesson learned: to do serious history it pays to dig deeper to discover new sources.

OK, this much I know. By the time Lincoln was making his speech at the Wisconsin State Fair the University had been up and running for eleven years. Who's in the audience? It's like asking who's buried in Grant's tomb. Farmers, but I'm beginning to think there was something different about some of the farmers listening to Lincoln: they might have been college educated. Or if they weren't maybe a relative or a friend was. Second Lesson: it's one thing to have a hypothesis it's another to find evidence that makes it plausible.

I found evidence to substantiate my hypothesis in the online version of *The University of Wisconsin 1848-1925* Vol. 1, written by Merle Curti and Vernon Carstensen, two historians who taught at Wisconsin. As the country was expanding during the 1840s there was a need for a new type of higher education, one that would train students in the practical arts like "scientific agriculture," civil engineering, and surveying. To meet this goal Wisconsin's Board of Regents created the "Department of the Practical Applications of Science." In establishing this department the Board envisioned farmers applying the latest methods, technology, and scientific knowledge to their crops, thereby improving productivity, increasing prosperity, and transforming farming into a profession. It became clear to me that Lincoln was addressing the converted. His message about forging bonds between agriculture, education, and free labor as a means of improving peoples' lives affirmed what was already happening in Wisconsin.

As I was looking up the University's founding date, another timeline entry caught my eye. In 1866 the state legislature designated the University as Wisconsin's land-grant institution under the Morrill Act. Although pre-occupied with the events of the Civil War, Congress nevertheless did manage to pass the Morrill Act in 1862. I think its passage, along with the enactment of the *Emancipation Proclamation,* is among the most transformative moments in American history.

The Morrill act basically changed the rules of the game for higher education by democratizing it. It made it possible for states to establish educational institutions that offered courses in practical science, agriculture, and engineering, using proceeds from the grant of federally owned land. By passing the Morrill Act, the national government made it possible for the sons of Wisconsin's farmers to attend college. Third Lesson: There's nothing like studying the past to give a person perspective. Even though the Morrill Act was passed by a Republican Congress and signed into law by a Republican president, today's GOP would dismiss it as just another example of big government abandoning any sense of limits. Even on the off chance the current Congress did pass it, Wisconsin's Republican governor would do his best to overturn it, in the name of balancing the budget.

What did college educated farmers have to do with James's Harvard? Plenty. If they and the sons of factory workers were the students of the future, how would a traditional school like Harvard thrive in this new educational and social order? The question was an urgent one. In 1861, the year nineteen-year-old James entered its Lawrence Scientific School, Harvard College had become an educational backwater. Even though the College clung to its traditional mission as the place where the virtues of service, piety, fortitude, prudence, and justice were instilled into the sons of the elite, in actuality it had degenerated into a type of reform school for the rich and powerful. Harvard College had become a place where teaching privileged boys how to behave eclipsed rigorous intellectual effort.

James Richardson describes the College's decline this way. "The curriculum was largely fixed and uninteresting, consisting mainly of the classics, taught by rote and examined by recitation. The boys considered it bad form for a student to talk to a teacher unless it was absolutely unavoidable. Frederic Hodge, a transcendentalist minister and friend of Emerson's, observed in 1866 that the college was not really a college at all but 'a more advanced school for boys,' the principle of which was coercion, the professors taskmasters and police officers, and the president the 'chief of the College police.' Religion— that is, Protestantism—ruled. The future historian John Fiske was docked sixty-four merit points in 1861-62, his junior year for reading the work of Auguste Comte during Sunday service in Christ Church. President C.C. Felton wrote Fiske's parents, threatening to expel the boy if he tried to spread his 'infidel' opinions."

After reading this I understood why James's father wouldn't allow William to go to any college. From Richardson's description, who would have thought that Harvard in the 1860s would become higher education's number one brand? Which brings me to Rule 4: Everything, even Harvard, has a history. Change is the only constant.

Charles W. Eliot wouldn't be surprised at Harvard's metamorphosis since he initiated the changes that set it into motion. I asked Ms. Jessup where I could find background information about Eliot and she introduced me to the American National Biography Online. I'm learning that a large part of independent study's challenge is to find sources that lead to others. I was lucky in this case. The entry on Eliot mentioned the two part article he wrote for the *Atlantic Monthly* in 1869 called "The New Education: Its Organization," which I found online. The other was *Between Harvard and America: The Educational Leadership of Charles W. Eliot*. I borrowed it from the Mid-Manhattan Branch of the NYPL.

I haven't had much time to read about Eliot, but the little I did made me think of about being an inside outsider. On the one hand you could say Harvard, during the nineteenth century, was the Eliot family business. Grandfather endowed a professorship, Charles's uncles were Harvard professors, two of his cousins were classmates, and his father published a history of the University and served as its treasurer. Given all his insider status as a member of the Eliot family, Charles as a person was an outsider. Even as a boy he was a loner and developed serious interests not typical for a son of Boston's elite. Charles was serious about science, particularly chemistry. In 1858 he became an assistant professor of math and chemistry at the Lawrence Scientific School where three years later he became James's teacher. That's as far as I've gotten. The question I'm left with is how did Eliot change Harvard so that a farmer's grandson who heard Lincoln's speech would want to go there and could.

I'm ashamed to admit it Doc, but following my nose in search of a book about Eliot was the first time I've used the public library since I was a little kid. Back then my baby-sitter or parents would take me to the Jefferson Street Branch for story hour and to borrow picture books. As I got older I didn't use it because I relied on Alden's library for books or I bought them. The other day was the first time I used the public library to track down specific information.

Entering the Mid-Manhattan Branch was a relief. It's like an oasis of quiet and calm amidst the noise and jostling of Fifth Avenue. Once inside I decided to look around. A sign and a display caught my attention. The sign said "Laptop Use for 45 Minutes." The display presented information about the impact 43 million dollars of proposed budget cuts would have if the City Council passed them. Next to that chart were petitions addressed to the Mayor and the City Council Speaker making the case for not slashing the library's budget. One set of petitions was for adults to sign; the other was written specifically for teenagers. Reading over the one for teens I was reminded of the huge role the neighborhood library plays in Luis's life. The bulk of what he reads comes from its collection, he does his homework there, he takes his siblings to story hour and uses its internet.

It was while I was thinking about the sign, the display, and Luis, that the difference between what's public and what's private became personal. 45 minutes on a Laptop is a joke. My school friends and I usually spend at least twenty minutes procrastinating before we get to work, reading email and checking our Facebook and Twitter accounts. We can do that because we own our laptops. That's when it hit me: private means owning the resources I need to accomplish what I want to do. If the laptop and the book are mine, I decide when and how to use them and for what purposes.

Public means resources are owned in common. In fact I'd go so far as to say politics is the process that involves people in deciding which resources will be designated as public, what their purposes are, who will have access to them and when. If the political system is a tyranny or absolute monarchy one person decides, if it's an oligarchy an elite determines what is public, if it's a democratic republic citizens acting through their representatives designate what's held in common.

This brings me back to Luis. He needs a strong public safety net so he can have access to those resources that I own. Ideally Luis needs a neighborhood library that is open 24/7, can distribute laptops to anyone with a library card, and has enough staff to teach members how to use the equipment. Since I'm thinking about the public resources Luis would need to have the same shot at Cornell as I do at Harvard, why stop at libraries? What about schools? Why all this talk about what's an excellent school. It seems pretty clear to me. Alden is an excellent school. We should do what it takes to make public education as good as any private school in the country. The goal would be to make private schools superfluous because the public ones would be outstanding. Radical? Sure, but is there a more effective way to make equality of opportunity more than a slogan in this country?

And here's the kicker. I realized that even the bubble's true believers benefit from a strong public safety net. I'm not talking about the obvious benefits like police and fire protection, sound roads and bridges, clean water, air, and good sanitation. I'm talking about what I saw when I crossed the street from the Mid-Manhattan Library and checked out the reading room in the Stephen Schwarzman Building. It dawned on me that even Mr. Schwarzman can't afford to own all the books, prints, photographs, and memorabilia that are housed within, off site, and underneath this beautiful building. Even he, along with the rest of the 1%, and the other 99% rely on this public institution for their cultural memories.

21. Doc Gives Citizen Emilia Something to Ponder

Dear Emilia,

Your experience at the library goes to the heart of some of the most important political questions of the day: What is a just distribution of goods and services within a democratic republic? Are there certain goods and services that should remain public and not be subject to privatization? If so, what is the fairest way to pay for them? What role, if any, should elites play in providing for the common good? How does increasing economic inequality affect the political life of a democratic republic? While these questions have been raised most recently by the Occupy movement, they will undoubtedly become key issues in the upcoming presidential race.

But there's a problem. In my opinion, politics in this country has become so polarized that these questions won't get the serious discussion they merit until unwavering party loyalty is no longer equated with political virtue and compromise with betrayal. To bring this about, Americans would need to retrieve a political vocabulary that enables us to recognize what we have in common. We would need to recover the language that enables us to think and talk about ourselves as a public.

You're right, it's easy to identify the qualities that make a school excellent—plenty of models exist. The difficult part is convincing persons with no reason for supporting public education to do so. How do you convince citizens, even those that don't have kids attending public school, that they are part of the public served by the public school system, and that it's in their best interest to share the responsibility for maintaining it?

To make the question more concrete: How would you persuade Alden's parents to pay higher taxes to support excellent public schools, libraries, day care centers, after school programs, and health care, in Luis's neighborhood? You could argue that by adding more to the public treasury, they would be making equality of opportunity less of a sham. But by providing the revenue to level the meritocratic playing field, they'd also be increasing the competition for privileges they believe their kids are entitled to. Why would any parent do that? To complicate matters even more, before you could argue your case for an all-out approach to school reform there are other political questions you'd need to address.

How are you going to counter the effect of a minority, you call them the bubble's true believers, whose self-interest is best served by polarizing the majority? The effect of this minority's power, wealth, and influence insures that the majority lacks the solidarity to recognize its own interests, let alone defend a public safety net.

How do you convince those who need a strong public safety net, but are disaffected from the political process that it's in their best interest to get involved and resist the forces that are intent on shredding it?

How do you create the conditions that would build trust among increasingly fractured and polarized constituencies making it possible for them to talk to one another about what they hold in common? How do you transform their responses into a political will that can affect change?

You've actually experienced some of the difficulties a lack of trust causes within a polarized society. Even though most of Luis's friends never met you, they nevertheless didn't trust you. And why should they? As far as they're concerned you're one of those rich, white, stuck-up do-gooders who has little or no knowledge of how they get through a day. Yet owing to your status you have the arrogance to think you understand their lived circumstances. As they saw it, you and your ideas would only create a mess that eventually they would have to live with.

Then there was the flip side—drumming up support for *The City as Educator* at school. At least the students at Alden knew you, and because of that they listened to what you had to say. But how do you get Luis's friends and Alden's students to move beyond their knee jerk mistrust of each other and engage in a dialogue that eventually might reveal common ground?

In a previous letter you mentioned that your schooling has consistently emphasized leadership and service. From what I observe, you want to understand how a member of the elite, dedicated to public discussion and interaction, best fulfills the roles of citizen and leader. That concern brings me back to William James. I think you'll find he had similar concerns. James became politically active during a period not unlike our own. The start of our century is sometimes called the second Gilded Age. James's lived most of his adult life during the first: a period like ours characterized by gross inequality, controversy over the nature of America's foreign commitments, polarization about the role of government, social fragmentation, rapid technological and scientific change.

Since you've begun to reflect on the meaning of citizenship, you might be interested to find out how James interpreted it. Let's consider this in finalizing the syllabus.

22. Becoming Acquainted with the Young Man from Wisconsin

Dear Doc,

Citizenship has been at the back of my mind lately and I'm looking forward to getting more deeply into it with James. The issue is personal because I'll be able to vote in my first presidential election this coming November and my Dad is involved with a local group that is protesting NYU 2031, the university's latest expansion plan. Listening to my father talk about how difficult it will be to get NYU to expand somewhere other than the West Village, I'm left wondering what, if any, influence the average citizen has these days. Aside from voting, jury duty, giving money to or working for a candidate, and protesting some policy, I don't think it's much. I hope I'm wrong.

But for now my attention is focused on Eliot, specifically the changes he initiated at Harvard that would make it possible for the grandson of a farmer to attend. I googled Harvard College Class of 1900 and found the Secretary's Report. Listed among the graduates was Kenneth McG. Martin a young man from Milwaukee, Wisconsin. Although Harvard in 1900 was still a college dominated by the eastern WASP elite, the young man from Wisconsin signaled a change.

Imagine that it's the start of the twentieth century and Kenny is making his way across Harvard Yard hurrying to class. He's unaware that the older man he just passed is Professor James. Our student is also unaware that the half-century of reforms President Eliot has overseen have changed Harvard College from an institution James's father found contemptible to the centerpiece of a modern university.

Kenny has made the train trip to Harvard ostensibly to put some distance between himself and Milwaukee. He's the odd one of the clan—never content, driven to make his own distinctive mark on the world—and he like Eliot is in love with all things scientific. Kenny is attending Harvard College because he believes his passion for science, whether applied or pure, will be welcomed there. Little does he know or care that this is a relatively new state of affairs.

Before then, when Eliot was James's chemistry instructor at Harvard's Lawrence Scientific School, it was considered even more of a backwater than the College. Basically if a student had reasonably good attendance he got a degree. One of the changes Eliot made was to encourage the pursuit of scientific knowledge within the College by merging Lawrence's faculty into the Faculty of Arts and Sciences; consequently all members of Lawrence's faculty became members of the College.

Even before he set foot on campus Kenny benefited from Eliot's reforms. He was admitted because he demonstrated proficiency in English, science, a modern language other than English, history, mathematics, and Latin—all subjects taught in his public high school in Milwaukee. What he didn't have to do was demonstrate proficiency in ancient Greek, a subject not taught back home. By 1894 Eliot had convinced Harvard's overseers that western civilization wouldn't crumble if Greek was no longer used as the gold standard for admission.

Not only did Kenny's present look promising due to President's Eliot's reforms, but so did his future. In 1906 owing to his commitment to strengthening scientific research at Harvard, President Eliot created The Graduate School of Applied Science. There our young man could continue his studies with the goal of producing some original research, earn a Doctorate in Science (the requirements for which were even more stringent than the Ph.D.), become an expert in his field, and even land a tenured position at Harvard or elsewhere. Not bad for a young man from Wisconsin, then or now.

Harvard admitted Kenny because he embodied its future. The revamped admissions requirements and the movement towards standardized testing that Eliot endorsed made it possible for students from a wider geographic area to apply and for Harvard to judge their merit. Because of where he came from, Kenny was one of the first participants in a slow, significant, and still evolving process—the diversifying of America's elite.

Under Eliot's leadership, the College was reinventing itself. Affirming intellectual rigor, public service, and excellence, Harvard College at the start of the twentieth century, served as an incubator for a new type of leader. The College prepared Boston Brahmin and Wisconsin provincial to embrace values associated with the professional. By the time Kenny entered graduate school he would be representative of a more democratic and meritocratic Harvard.

If Kenny and I could erase the century that separates us, I think he would recognize the Harvard I applied to. His was its first modern incarnation, mine its latest. But you know Doc, it's what went before that interests and baffles me. Granted all I have to go on is a book about Eliot and one on James, but each depicts the traditional college, with its prescribed curriculum based on the classics and the Bible, as an ineffective relic. From these readings I get the impression that the traditional college's mission, to instill character, was a throwback to the days when Harvard's student body was made up of a small, insular, elite secure in its status. In these books Eliot is depicted as an academic crusader who with foresight, courage, and determination modernizes the College, replacing the prescribed curriculum with the elective system and opening up its admission policy to academically gifted boys from the hinterlands.

Yes, but. Doc, have you seen the animated film "Wall-E"? The story takes place after an ecological disaster has forced humanity to leave earth and take up residence on floating space stations. Wall-E is a robotic trash compactor who has remained on earth and continues to do his job after everyone has left. When he's not compacting, Wall-E tries to piece together what life was like on earth before the disaster struck. The only clues he has are bits of trash he collects: Zippo lighters, a Rubik's cube, and a "Hello Dolly!" videotape. From these he cobbles together an interpretation of modern life that resembles a Fred Astaire Ginger Rogers movie.

I feel like Wall-E when it comes to understanding Harvard College before Eliot. Like the robot I don't have much to go on, only Eliot's side of the story. I suspect the traditional college had more going for it than its critics acknowledged, but I haven't a clue as to what that was.

23. Nuts and Bolts

Dear Emilia,

As a matter of fact I've seen "Wall-E" and thought the movie could be an allegory for doing serious history. Both Wall-E and the historian confront the challenge of piecing together a creditable portrait of the past with a collection of sources that is often incomplete, contradictory, and sometimes accidentally misleading. And like Wall-E, the historian keeps looking for the source that will clearly and eloquently shed light on what went on before. For your purposes the *Yale Report of 1828* fits that description. It provides a more nuanced description of the traditional college than the one advanced by its critics, and disputes the portrayal of it by James 's father as the ruination of young men. You might even find yourself agreeing with some of the arguments its authors make.

Now to the nuts and bolts. Here's the syllabus for the semester. If this were a no-holds-barred independent study you'd be responsible for devising a schedule of required readings and a bibliography of supplemental materials. Since study is long, time is short, and you're new at this, I took your suggestions and devised what I think is a reasonable undertaking. My revisions shouldn't prohibit you from making additions, but given that we are talking about three and a half months, I think these essays elegantly and economically address your interests.

Because our time is limited, I think it best to concentrate on your more immediate concerns—James's ideas about education and Harvard. Towards that end, I've added two essays— "The Proposed Shortening of the College Course" and "The True Harvard"—and I've removed *Pragmatism* from the list. James delivered those lectures to sophisticated listeners, trying to ground a complex set of ideas that were too rapidly becoming an academic fad. The work is much more difficult than it appears, and to be blunt, at this stage of your academic life, you lack the necessary philosophic background to engage it well within the time limits of the semester. So, instead of getting bogged down in a work you're not ready to grapple with, I've substituted James's essay, "The Moral Equivalent of War." Reading this, you'll get a sense of where James would have stood vis-à-vis Dewey versus Bourne on the Great War.

On finishing "The Ph.D. Octopus," you raised the question—When, if ever, did James's vision of the university "... as the jealous custodian of personal and spiritual spontaneity" ever flourish? In response, I've included a substantial excerpt from the *Yale Report of 1828*, which may deepen the question further. I also added James's "Address on the Medical Registration Bill" (1898) because it foreshadows the concerns he took up in "The Ph.D. Octopus."

Fortunately most of James's work is on the net, and the Emory site you found is a good one. I've identified the more obscure essays with an asterisk and you can pick copies of them up at the office. As to secondary sources I'll suggest them as the need arises. Mondays after school would be the most convenient time to meet. If there's a problem feel free to come by any Monday. If all is well, I've set aside the first Monday in March, April and May for conversations in real time.

As to the written requirement, what about incorporating your thoughts, questions, and criticisms about James's essays in subsequent letters? They would provide a comfortable framework for recording your engagement with his work, especially as it pertains to the issues that emerged last semester. As you read James, ask yourself how he would interpret the purpose of an education, particularly a college education, the role an elite plays in a democracy, and the significance of the inner life in a modern society. By the time May rolls around you might not have the answers, but you will have a chronicle of your study. I can't think of a better graduation gift than that.

INDEPENDENT STUDY SCHEDULE
EMILIA CARLYLE

Readings

To be completed by Monday, March 5

> "The Yale Report 1828"
> "The Proposed Shortening of the College Course" (1891)*
> "Address on the Medical Registration Bill" (1898)*
> "The Ph.D. Octopus" (1903)
> "The True Harvard" (1903)

To be completed by Monday, April 2

> "The Social Value of the College Bred" (1907)
> "The Moral Equivalent of War" (1910)

To be completed by Monday, May 5

> *Talks to Students* (1892)
> "The Gospel of Relaxation"
> "On a Certain Blindness In Human Beings"
> "What Makes A Life Significant"

24. For Emilia the Issue Is One of Character

Dear Doc,

Your idea of continuing to write letters into the second semester is fine with me. Since starting this project, I'm beginning to think I'm channeling some nineteenth century version of myself. Before we began writing to each other, texting and tweeting were as close to letter writing as I got. Now I actually enjoy putting pen to paper, and much to my parents delight no longer procrastinate about writing thank you notes. Like the slow food movement, maybe I should start a slow communication movement. Also, thanks for finding some of the readings for me and setting aside time to meet face-to-face. At this point in my schooling, I appreciate having an independent study equipped with training wheels.

For about a day I believed I had this independent study wrapped up. I thought I'd found the institution that tried to act as the guardian of the inner life. It was right there in the "Yale Report of 1828," and I have to admit I became somewhat of a fan. To be more precise I came to admire the importance the defenders of the traditional college placed on character and their determination to maintain an education that developed it. For all of the traditional college's shortcomings about how to build character like—the prescribed curriculum, mandatory chapel, demerit systems—at least it took character seriously. Its defenders envisioned the traditional college as a place where a student disciplined and furnished his mind so that he could go out into the world with "a proper balance of character." And the "Report" clearly stated that it's a student's responsibility to rely on the ". . . resources of his own mind," in order to ". . . form himself by his own exertions." Isn't that just what we've been talking about and exactly what today's college student doesn't do?

My grandfather who loves history has a favorite saying, "history is written by the winners." I was thinking about that after finishing a large chunk of the "Report." I began to see Eliot's reforms in a different light. Eliot was the winner when it came to designing the college's future. Today his reforms have become the way things are and ought to be. But when he was instituting his changes, he defended them on the grounds that they would succeed in accomplishing what the traditional college failed to do—build character in its undergraduates. Isn't it ironic that Eliot and his supporters had to demolish the traditional college to accomplish its mission? But as far as I'm concerned they failed too.

What college today, possibly other than a religious one, sets out to attract prospective students by claiming to build character? I've recently seen a lot of college web sites and am assured I can go to college to build friendships, contacts, interests, confidence, success, and competence, but character not so much. I think even mentioning character and college in the same sentence makes a current high school student suspicious. She half expects that character is a cover for some form of indoctrination the college is hatching. I applied to eight colleges and in their mission statements phrases such as "the pursuit of excellence," "learning broadly and deeply," and "freeing the mind to its fullest potential," are tossed out, but no mention of the C word. The closest I came to finding a statement that alluded to character was "leading principled lives of consequence." But that phrasing gives the impression that character matters only as long as it leads to success and influence. I've yet to see a category labeled "character development" in the *US News and World Report* college ranking issue.

As I looked at "The Proposed Shortening of the College Course" and decided to read it the next day, I figured that James would be against it. I assumed this to be the case because of what I took away from the only other essay of his I had read—"The Ph.D. Octopus." James was worried about the character issue. He observed that all the new degrees being offered as part of the expansion of graduate education were

making it increasingly difficult for people to distinguish between expertise and character. Individuals mistakenly associated the credential with good character when its actual purpose was to indicate expertise and merit. Concerned about this
confusion, why would James support the shortening of Harvard's college course if the college were the one place in the
university where something like the education of character
occurred? I went to bed convinced that James, although a Harvard man of long standing, would nevertheless demonstrate
nobility of character and side with the old Yalies of 1828.

Boy did I get it wrong! Not only did James support shortening undergraduate education from four to three years, but
he did so on the grounds that it would prevent the corruption
of character. Most college students, he argued, were intelligent
but not interested in theory. Three years was more than
enough time for them to broaden their intellectual outlook.
Any more time spent in the classroom would result in, "List-
lessness, apathy, dawdling, sauntering, the smoking of ciga-
rettes and living on small sarcasms, the 'Harvard indifference,'
in short, of which outsiders have so frequently complained are
the direct fruit of keeping these men too long from that world
of affairs to which they rightfully belong." Even though I'm
not sure cutting a year out of college would eradicate the Harvard indifference, I am certain its twenty-first century version
is alive and well and has expanded beyond Cambridge. It's the
attitude of the bright and bored best summed up in the phrase
"been there done that," and the word "whatever."

Reading the "Yale Report" and James's "The Proposed
Shortening of the College Course," I noticed that both the defenders of the traditional college and James, writing on behalf
of its critics, championed a type as their model for a man of
character. For the authors of the "Report" it was the gentleman,
a person who went to college to broaden his perspective as
preparation for the leadership role he would assume by virtue
of his birth. Freed from the necessity of having to earn a living,
he was in no hurry to graduate and could take his time getting
what the "Report" called a "thorough" education before decid-

ing on a vocation. As prescribed by the college his course of study would be what we'd call a liberal arts education—mathematics, physical science, ancient literature, English reading (which would be like today's English Composition), philosophy, rhetoric, and oratory. The defenders of the traditional college assumed learning those subjects would ". . . give that expansion and balance of the mental powers, those liberal and comprehensive views, and those fine proportions of character, which are not to be found in him whose ideas are always confined to one particular channel."

For the defenders of the traditional college the threat to it and to the character of an undergraduate was specialized knowledge, the type of knowledge we call professional. As they saw it, to turn a young man into a professional before he had adequate time to develop breath and discipline of mind is to deform his character. He will for the remainder of his life be regarded ". . . as a man of limited views and attainments." And there are public consequences whenever a young man is transformed into a professional before he's ripe. The public will be deprived of a leader who sees beyond the immediate, the contingent, and his self-interest, and can act according to the principles of good stewardship for the common good.

The authors of the "Yale Report" asked: "Can merchants, manufacturers, and agriculturists, derive no benefit from high culture? . . . Is it not desirable that they should be men of superior education, of large and liberal views, of those solid and elegant attainments, which will raise them to a higher distinction, than the mere possession of property; which will not allow them to hoard their treasures, or waste them in senseless extravagance; which will enable them to adorn society by their learning, to move in the more intelligent circles with dignity, and to make such an application of their wealth, as will be most honorable to themselves, and most beneficial to their country?"

After reading this inspiring depiction of the great and the good, the best and the brightest, I had an epiphany. I realized how to narrow the wealth gap between the 1 and the 99%.

Forget tax reform, investing in new technologies and infra-structure, or making sure corporations pay their fair share. The best solution is to convince the 1% to learn Greek and Latin. It could become the next new status symbol even surpassing the Mandarin nanny on the bling index. Think of it! One-percenters from Southampton to Beverly Hills reading Aristo-tle's *Ethics* in the original. In no time the minimum wage would quadruple, public institutions—everything from schools to parks—would be awash in cash, and as my history loving grandfather would say, "sure, when pigs fly."

James would say "bosh." Bosh to the traditional college's insistence on offering a prescribed curriculum, bosh to its four year duration, bosh to its determination to protect undergrad-uates from the alleged corruptive influence of specialized knowledge, and bosh to the traditional college's gentleman as the exemplar of character. It was all bosh as far as James was concerned because the traditional college charmed its defend-ers by offering up a "golden and dreamy and amateurish ideal" that couldn't stand up to "the fighting side of life" and was inferior ". . . as an agent in the formation of character to that more strenuous and professional sort of ideal, which our [Harvard's] recent reforms have tended to consolidate." For James and the reformers the professional ideal improved the tone of the college by dissipating the Harvard indifference. The students, James observed, were "maturer; you meet them more as equals, you expect more and get more from them, and can appeal to their cooperation as a matter of course, in ways which formerly might have proved disappointing experi-ments."

I say bosh to both exemplars of character—the gentleman and the professional. I agree with James that the traditional college's portrait of the gentleman as steward of the public good was a fantasy. But James's depiction of the serious, ac-complished, and service-minded professional, I find equally hard to swallow. Doc, I know I'm guilty of presentism, but it's difficult for me to take James's position seriously. When I think of professionals I think of individuals whose ideal of service begins and ends with themselves.

I don't know if my generation has an exemplar of character. If we do maybe it's the entrepreneur. Unlike the professional, the entrepreneur doesn't have to follow the rules of some bloated bureaucracy, she establishes her own—she innovates. Listening to the usual suspects—politicians, CEOs, and pundits—I get the impression that innovation is this year's magic word for making the future bright. This brings me to Emilia's history lesson #5. Considering all the types that were and are supposed to exemplify character—the gentleman, the professional, and the entrepreneur—I've concluded that one generation's progress is another generation's problem.

One last thing. There's something about James's support of the professional ideal that doesn't add up. Why in "The Proposed Shortening of the College Course," would he be so supportive of it and then in "The Ph. D. Octopus" sound the alarm about the system that certifies professionals? Maybe after I've read the other three essays in this section I'll understand what caused James to have second thoughts about specialization, professionalism, and credentialing thirteen years later.

25. Doc Counsels Emilia to Keep Complexity in Mind as She Investigates Character

February 13

Dear Emilia,

Your suggestion concerning innovation as this year's magic word prompted me to remember another. The year was 1967, the word was plastics, and the movie was *The Graduate*. If you haven't seen it, I think you'd enjoy it. The scene that comes to mind is one where Ben's parents are hosting a party to celebrate his graduation from college. Mr. McGuire, a family friend, corrals Ben and tells him he has one word to say, just one word—plastics. He advises Ben that there's a great future in plastics, and that he should think about it.

✗ Following Mr. McGuire's lead, I have one word for you, as you anticipate your high school graduation, just one word—complexity. Unlike innovation and plastics, complexity won't ensure a brilliant and bountiful future, but it's a helpful word to keep in mind as you read James and try to understand his views about character in general and his character in particular.

One way to think about study is as an activity that seeks out and discloses the complexity and nuance of its subject. Unfortunately, attending to complexity and nuance has rarely✗ been a priority on most peoples' to-do list. I think that's particularly evident these days when proclaiming fast, facile, and superficial answers to trite questions gives a person her fifteen minutes of fame. A culture like ours, fueled by the mind ✗ numbing duet of celebrity and crisis, generates an atmosphere in which a person trying to grapple with a subject in all its complexity is often accused of flip flopping. For a significant ✗ segment of the population, a person who changes her mind is perceived as weak willed and duplicitous. The idea that changing one's mind indicates intellectual complexity, growth and self-correction is heresy.

Probably James's time was no more accepting of complexity and nuance than ours, but fortunately he relished both. As the person studying James, it might be helpful to think of yourself as a cartographer of his mental landscape. Because you are getting to know a complex person be prepared to explore an inner life that is eclectic, variable, often contradictory, occasionally wild, and even mysterious. Sounds like a trip worth taking.

Here are two signposts that will help you chart your course. The first is from "The Ph. D. Octopus." It's one of those sentences that at first doesn't make much of an impression, but in subsequent readings it might help you make sense of James's apparent ambivalence about professionalism.

"But the institutionalizing on a large scale of any natural combination of need and motive always tends to run into technicality and to develop a tyrannical Machine with unforeseen powers of exclusion and corruption."

The second signpost is an excerpt from a letter James wrote to a family friend, Mrs. Henry Whitman, June 7, 1899.

"I am against bigness and greatness in all their forms, and with the invisible molecular forces that work from individual to individual, stealing in through crannies of the world like so many soft rootlets, or like the capillary oozing of water, and yet rending the hardest monuments of man's pride, if you give them time. The bigger the unit you deal with, the hollower, the more brutal, the more mendacious is the life displayed. So I am against all big successes and big results; and in favor of eternal forces of truth which always work in the individual and immediately unsuccessful way, under-dogs always, till history comes, after they are long dead, and puts them on top. —You need take no notice of these ebullitions of spleen, which are probably quite unintelligible to anyone but myself."

26. Character's Corrupters, or Bigness and the Club Opinion

February 22

Dear Doc,

I get it! It all makes sense! I understand why James was a cheerleader for professionalism in 1898 and a critic of it in 1903. It's because of the controversy over the Medical Registration Bill, his abhorrence of bigness and his devotion to the individual.

Going on nothing other than the bill's name I assumed James supported it. The idea that he wouldn't seemed preposterous to me. Who would go to a doctor who wasn't board certified? I've never heard of a legitimate one who wasn't. I'll even admit that as far as the credentialing mania is concerned, it's fine with me when it comes to medical schools. The more diplomas and certificates of commendation that decorate my doctor's office the securer I feel. Whenever my parents have had to find a physician, they'd get recommendations from friends and then research those suggestions on line. Board certification is usually the first category listed on any website that ranks and provides information about doctors.

Again I got James wrong. When I thought he'd oppose the shortening of the college course, he supported it. When I assumed he'd support the licensing of Massachusetts doctors he opposed it. At first I thought his position demonstrated perversity rather than complexity. How could someone who earned a medical degree from Harvard, taught Anatomy and Physiology and created the Psychology Department be against this bill? James pulled no punches answering my question. It's because he was dedicated to science that he saw ". . . in this bill (along with some good intentions) a movement in favor of ignorance."

What connection does James see between the Medical Registration Bill and ignorance? The purpose of the bill was twofold. Its first aim was to have doctors in Massachusetts pass a state administered examination in order to obtain a license to practice. Its second, related aim was to put unorthodox practitioners the medical profession labeled mind-curers—homeopaths, Christian Scientists, hypnotists, and mediums—out of business. The members of the Massachusetts Medical Society assumed that no self-respecting mind-curer would agree to take its examination. From the Society's perspective, passing the bill would rid Massachusetts of this scourge because it transformed the mind curers' quackery into a crime. As I read the background to the bill I couldn't see why James was making an issue out of what seemed to me a common sense policy. Wasn't the licensing of doctors good for the public and for the profession?

James answered with a resounding no. He argued that even if the intention of the bill was to protect the public from quacks, the public would nevertheless seek them out because, "Their movement is a religious or quasi-religious movement: personality is one condition of success there, and impressions and intuitions seem to accomplish more than chemical, anatomical or physiological information." The other reason James thought the bill wouldn't contribute to the public good was it allowed the state to meddle in an area where it had no expertise. ". . . the Commonwealth of Massachusetts is not a medical body, has no right to a medical opinion, and should not dare to take sides in medical controversies." I thought that was a lame argument and wrote in the margin "yeah, tell that to the FDA." Then I remembered there was no FDA in 1898. While checking out its founding date, 1906, I also discovered that althhough founded in 1847, the AMA wasn't incorporated until 1897.

That's when your signposts kicked in. As I see it, James's fight against the bill was in part a fight against sacrificing one's autonomy to the agencies, bureaucracies, corporations, institutions, and professions he believed were rapidly taking over and reconfiguring human life on a scale that dwarfed the individual, threatened to make her superfluous, and corrupt her character. By opposing the bill James was resisting the ". . . tyrannical Machine with unforeseen powers of exclusion and corruption" as well as its energizing sources—bigness and greatness. What alarmed him was his contemporaries' eagerness to equate bigness with progress and ignore its cultural costs. That cost was ignorance.

James called the ignorance associated with bigness "the Club-opinion," and its effect was to deprive the medical profession of potentially important therapeutic knowledge for the sake of professional solidarity. James brought this to light when he asked, "How many of my learned medical friends, who today are so freely denouncing mind-cure methods as an abominable superstition, have taken the pains to follow up the cases of some mind-curer, one by one, so as to acquaint themselves with the results? I doubt if there be a single individual. 'Of such experience as that,' they say, 'give me ignorance rather than knowledge.' And the Club-opinion of the Massachusetts Medical Society pats them on the head and backs them up."

For the club opinion to dominate an organization it has to stroke the vanity of its members. James revealed how this "not wholly evil" practice begins. "I don't blame any set of practitioners for remaining ignorant of all practice but their own. The subject is too overwhelmingly great. It takes an entire life to gain adequate experience of a few diseases and a few remedial methods. When a doctor notes what he considers good effects from his own practice, it is natural for him to let well enough alone, and refrain from exploring unknown lines."

But then he described how this narrowing of focus metastasizes into the club opinion and corrupts character. "But when ignorance and narrowness, instead of being humble, grow insolent and authoritative, and ask for laws whose only immediate result can be to perpetuate them, then I think every citizen interested in the growth of a genuinely complete medical science should rise up and protest." Simply change the date of James's address and substitute Lehman Brothers, AIG, banks too big to fail, BP, Penn State, or Congress for the Massachusetts Medical Society and James's description of the club opinion, I'd call it group think, is as accurate today as it was when he wrote it.

This brings me to "The True Harvard." James made it clear that even a college was susceptible to the club opinion if the "idealization of 'success' in the mere outward sense of 'getting there,' and getting there on as big a scale as we can . . ." is the prime reason for attending. If that's the case, then, according to James, the student acquires an "educated cleverness in the service of popular idols and vulgar ends." But later in the talk, James observed that Harvard College or any other institution of higher learning can resist becoming promoters of the club opinion by offering sanctuary for exceptionality and eccentricity owing to ". . . her devotion to the principles of individual vocation and choice." For James that's the purpose of the true Harvard.

If, for James, resistance against bigness, greatness, and the ignorance they perpetuate came down to the principles of individual vocation and choice, then what does a person need to know to take on that struggle? In what I've read so far, James doesn't answer that question. However, I suspect the answer has something to do with cultivating character because James ends his speech with a warning, "The day when Harvard shall stamp a single hard and fast type of character upon her children, will be that of her downfall." Not from what I observe. Isn't being branded "Harvard tested and approved" most peoples' idea of a dream come true?

Frankly Doc, I don't see the connection between a liberal arts education and getting the inner strength to resist the club opinion, whether that attitude takes hold in a college, a profession, or a co-op board. How does studying organic chemistry or rocks for jocks help a girl say no to group think and yes to knowing herself?

27. Doc Draws an Analogy between Working-Out and Exercising Reason

Dear Emilia,

Why can't you see a direct connection between a liberal arts education and becoming who you want to be, what the authors of the *Yale Report* and James call developing a character? Simple, there isn't any. Character isn't learned by taking a particular course. It develops out of the countless decisions, significant and not, a person makes to shape her life. Rather than a cause and effect relation between the liberal arts and character, there exists a link between the two owing to their shared relation with reason. The liberal arts are responsible for educating reason and reason, in turn, is character's seedbed. That said, it makes sense for us to explore reason as a means of understanding the link between a liberal arts education and character.

Most of the time when reason is mentioned, particularly around Alden, it's critical reason that's discussed. That label doesn't tell you much. But when you think of critical reason as thinking critically, it becomes more meaningful. Whereas critical reason is an abstraction floating in the conceptual stratosphere, thinking critically is usually tethered to something concrete. You can think critically about today's lunch choices, whether to confront the person who is spreading rumors about you, or which candidate to vote for in the upcoming presidential election. The other meaning people generally assign to reason is that of the mental faculty they depend on to get out of a predicament, to solve a problem, to get something done—reason in its instrumental mode.

The reason associated with the liberal arts, however, is more multi-faceted than our present usage indicates. It's reason as the discipline of the mind. The *Yale Report* provides the best description of this interpretation of reason I've read. Reason as the discipline of the mind is ". . . the art of fixing the attention, directing the train of thought, analyzing a subject proposed for investigation; following with accurate discrimination, the course of an argument; balancing nicely the evidence presented to judgment; awakening, elevating, and controlling the imagination; arranging, with skill, the treasures which memory gathers: rousing and guiding the powers of genius."

Unfortunately at this point in time, you and I might be among a handful of people, other than educational historians, who know that the *Report* exists. Its obscurity can be attributed, as your grandfather observed, to history being written by the winners. In this case Eliot's elective system triumphed over the *Report's* prescribed curriculum, causing the later to take a plunge into history's version of the Bermuda Triangle. Having faded from cultural memory, the *Report's* broad and rich interpretation of reason has also gone missing.

To better understand the *Report's* description of reason I came up with the following analogy: judgment is to mind as fitness is to body. No I don't want to resurrect memories of the analogy section of the SAT, but I know sports is one of your passions and thought this analogy was a good way to make a discussion of the reason associated with the liberal arts more comprehensible.

As a member of the soccer team you are undoubtedly aware of the different ways you can build up your muscles' capacities. One way is to make changes in your daily routine: take the stairs instead of the elevator, walk or bike rather than get on a bus. Another way is to set aside specific times during the week when you go to the gym to work out. Now imagine that your goal is to build up your reason's capacities. Like muscle it can be strengthened through the everyday decision-making you do. Or like going to the gym, where time and space is dedicated to physical conditioning, attending college offers similar opportunities for toning your reason.

As someone who knows her way around a gym you are undoubtedly familiar with the variety of equipment that's available—free weights, resistance machines, tread mills, mats, pool. Each has its specific purpose. Some equipment increases muscle strength; others improve endurance, balance, or flexibility. Well, think of the various subjects included in a liberal arts education as the equipment a person uses to improve her reason's fitness. The *Yale Report* explained how that works. "From the pure mathematics, he [the student] learns the art of demonstrative reasoning. In attending to the physical sciences, he becomes familiar with facts, with the process of induction, and the varieties of probable evidence. In ancient literature, he finds some of the most finished models for taste. By English reading, he learns the powers of the language in which he is to speak and write. By logic and mental philosophy, he is taught the art of thinking; by rhetoric and oratory, the art of speaking. By frequent exercise on written composition, he acquires copiousness and accuracy of expression. By extemporaneous discussion, he becomes prompt, and fluent, and animated."

For those of us who are not professional athletes, the purpose of going to the gym is to attain a level of fitness that gives a person a sense of well-being. That sense emerges from the confidence that one's body can meet the physical demands that come with the day. It's not all that different with the liberal arts and reason.

Ultimately the purpose of a liberal arts education is to build a person's confidence in her ability to meet the day's intellectual demands by educating her reason to make sound judgments about her lived circumstances.

It's not difficult to recognize a sound body. It's a body whose systems—respiratory, muscular, skeletal, digestive, nervous, reproductive, circulatory, and endocrine—work together making it possible for a person to marshal the energy and strength needed to accomplish her purposes. We watch a fit person move through her day displaying an unselfconscious ease, assured she can meet the spectrum of physical challenges that confront her.

A sound mind also has certain distinguishing features. Like the well-toned body it too is the sum of its parts. In this case the parts we're talking about aren't biological systems but are the mental faculties—reason, passion and the will. The liberal arts exercises reason so it's strong enough to harness the passions and the will to itself, thereby enabling all three faculties to work in concert. Just as co-ordination characterizes the fit body, it's also an attribute of the sound mind. A person's passions ignite her desire to aspire towards a purpose, her reason guides the effort she makes towards achieving it, and her will marshals the determination to sustain the effort. You might say a sound judgment is one in which the three faculties are in balance, much like one's health depends on a finely calibrated and changing balance among the body's systems. It brings to mind the ancient phrase, "a sound mind in a sound body."

The fitness of a person's judgments or lack thereof creates the foundation for her actions in the world. Over time, the sum of those actions is what is recognized as character. Character, along with "The Ph.D. Octopus," and "The True Harvard" was much on James's mind in 1903. In May of that year James gave an address to commemorate another renowned Harvard alum, Ralph Waldo Emerson. What James most admired about Emerson the man, the thinker, and the writer was his unshakeable commitment to the struggle each of us wages in order to recognize who we want to become, to cultivate our character. James reminded those assembled that in his writings Emerson admonished his reader to: "Trust thyself, every heart vibrates to that iron string. There is a time in each man's education when he must arrive at the conviction that imitation is suicide; when he must take himself for better or worse as his portion; and know that though the wide universe is full of good, no kernel of nourishing corn can come to him but through his toil bestowed on that plot of ground which it was given him to till." For James, Emerson's charge to trust thyself was the means a person deployed to resist the ignorance that bigness generated, the club opinion he abhorred. James also recognized how difficult that was. For many, to trust themselves based on the strength of their character is too lonely and terrifying an undertaking.

But nevertheless persons do trust themselves. In a tribute James wrote for his friend Thomas Davidson, also in 1903, James described the effect character has on others. "The memory of Davidson will always strengthen my faith in personal freedom and its spontaneities, and make me less unqualifiedly respectful than ever of Civilization with its herding and branding, licensing and degree-giving, authorizing and appointing, and in general regulating and administering by system the lives of human beings."

Isn't that somewhat similar to the feeling you have when you think about Ms. Basso, Mr. Thompson, and Doc O'Riley? Earlier in the year we called the quality these teachers embody integrity. James called it character. Either way, witnessing someone who acts according to what she has judged to be true, good, and/or beautiful opens up the definition of what it means to lead a human and humane life—enriching the possibilities for conducting our lives. Why does witnessing character have this effect? It reminds a person that at the root of her humanity is the potential for exercising the freedom to overturn the expected and to bring something new into the world.

Earlier in the year we took up the topic of back-stories and their importance for getting a more complex and nuanced understanding of a person or a topic. That certainly applies to the liberal arts. Its back-story starts with the ancient Greeks who defined the liberal arts as the education worthy of a free man. For our meeting next week let's talk about that definition and if it makes any sense in today's world.

28. To Know a Good Man When You See One

Dear Doc,

Let me see if I've gotten this straight. Before our meeting I thought a liberal arts education made a person free. Free in the sense of what we've been discussing—using reason to form judgments and acting accordingly. Now I understand that I had it backwards. Starting with the Greeks, a liberal arts education was the education of a person who was already free, free in the sense of thinking and acting for oneself—not taking direction from others. Usually that kind of freedom required a person to have wealth and status. That's why a liberal arts education became synonymous with the education of an elite. But riches and connections aren't necessarily prerequisites for becoming liberally educated. Socrates, as you pointed out was a relatively poor man, but nevertheless took responsibility for what he thought—as did Frederick Douglass and Phyllis Wheatley.

But generally the original liberal arts student was a wealthy male Athenian citizen with the leisure to discipline his mind. He didn't have to worry about earning a living or running a household; women and slaves did that. As for his future plans that was already determined. It was expected that he would fulfill his adult responsibilities as a member of the city's political elite. Time slightly altered the standard description of the liberal arts student; his slaves were eventually replaced by servants, but overall it endured for centuries.

What I took away from our discussion is that the conditions that spawned and sustained the liberal arts don't exist anymore and I say good riddance. But two millennia later, we're still talking about the liberal arts as the gold standard for a college education. Why? Something changed that prevented the liberal arts from becoming a relic. But what?

I might be way off here, but I think it goes back to reason, specifically, who is capable of exercising reason as the discipline of the mind. Here's the way I figure it. If as the *Yale Report* says the two purposes of a liberal education are to provide "the *discipline* and *furniture* of the mind; expanding its powers, and storing it with knowledge," then one has to assume that the person who is being liberally educated has a mind capable of being disciplined and furnished, that he's a rational human being. What's changed is that the entire slog towards modernity has been about including more and diverse people in that category. In fact, I'd argue that's modernity's defining feature.

All you have to do is follow the history of the franchise in this country. Casting a vote is to demonstrate publicly that you are capable of thinking rationally. First the vote was restricted to white men with property, then white men without property were included, next black men, and finally women. Even with much backsliding, like Jim Crow, the impetus was to move towards a more inclusive definition of citizenship and to diversify the category of people recognized as rational. Great, a more diverse group of people can vote. But except for voting, the majority of citizens living in a modern nation, unlike their Athenian counterparts living in the polis, don't actively participate in its public life. So I am left with this question: Is there a modern connection between the private purpose of a liberal education, the cultivation of one's character and a public purpose that makes sense in the twenty-first century?

Fortunately I didn't have long to wait for an answer. It was right there in "The Social Value of the College Bred": "to know a good man when you see him." At first I thought James was being ironic. No college mission statement I've ever read even comes close to stating that as one of its aims, let alone the aim. But as I got into the essay I realized James should be taken at his word.

In "The Social Value of the College Bred," James fitted the liberal arts to modern life. First off he renamed them. Throughout the essay he referred to the liberal arts as the humanities. In and of itself that's no big deal, except the name change is more than cosmetic for James. He also changes the criteria for defining a particular subject as liberal/humanistic. Whereas Yale's prescribed curriculum had about eight subjects that qualified as liberal, James believed "You can give humanistic value to almost anything by teaching it historically. Geology, economics, mechanics, are humanities when taught with reference to the successive achievements of the geniuses to which these sciences owe their being. Not taught thus, literature remains grammar, art a catalogue, history a list of dates, and natural science a sheet of formulas and weights and measures." For James a subject became humanistic when it was taught as a record of human effort.

James agreed with the authors of the *Yale Report* on one important point: a humanistic education disciplines the mind enabling a person to judge soundly. But James went a step further. He actually described what judging soundly entailed. "What the colleges—teaching humanities by examples which may be special, but must be typical and pregnant—should at least try to give us, is a general sense of what, under various disguises *superiority* has always signified and may signify. The feeling for a good human job anywhere, the admiration of the really admirable, the disesteem of what is cheap and trashy and impermanent—that is what we call the critical sense, the sense for ideal values. It is the better part of what men know as wisdom."

So putting all the pieces together I come up with this: According to James the purpose of the humanities is to enable a person to judge what are better and worse efforts made by himself and others in order to recognize what's excellent. And if character is the sum of a person's efforts, then the purpose of liberal/humanistic education is like James says, "to know a good man when you see him."

My initial reaction was—how elitist is that? Who am I to say what efforts made by others are better or worse? Isn't being judgmental wrong because it turns a person into a snob? But then I realized I make judgments about my own efforts and others' all the time. Who's the best physics teacher? Will doing this make any difference? Who's the best person to talk to about this question? What do I have to do to ace the test? What do I have to do to be admitted to this college? It dawned on me that it's not the actual act of judging someone or some effort better or worse that's elitist, it's the standards used to make those judgments that make it so.

It seems like a no brainer: a person making a judgment knows the standards she's using. After reading James, I'm beginning to suspect that's not the case. When it comes to making judgments, most folks, me included, go into default mode and latch onto standards that are culturally handy, what James called the club opinion. Right now those would be the big three: success, wealth, and status. Using them to judge what constitutes superior effort inevitably ends up disqualifying 99.9% of the population. How many people are high profile billionaires? But there's an upside to being a member of the club when it comes to judging what matters. At least success, wealth, and status make categorizing people simple. Either you are a winner or a loser based on your cash value.

But those standards tell us nothing about excellence of effort because they leave out an important component—why a person is making the effort in the first place. That entails judging what matters, which is another way of talking about recognizing one's purposes. Even the masters of the universe know this. Why else would they spend precious energy making heart felt attempts to wrap their pursuit of success, wealth, and status in the cloak of noble purposes like creating jobs, protecting the national interest, preserving American values, restoring religious values, supporting property rights, freeing the market, promoting the entrepreneur, speaking for the consumer, spreading democracy, maintaining the peace.

For me the most important part of "The Social Value of the College Bred" was James's description of the ways that studying the humanities broadens and deepens a person's standards for judging excellence. "All our arts and sciences and institutions are but so many quests of perfection on the part of men; and when we see how diverse the types of excellence may be, how various the tests, how flexible the adaptations, we gain a richer sense of what the terms "better" and "worse" may signify in general. Our critical sensibilities grow both more acute and less fanatical. We sympathize with men's mistakes even in the act of penetrating them; we feel the pathos of lost causes and misguided epochs even while we applaud what overcame them."

After reading this passage I finally understood why my version of *The City as Educator* project was both a failure and not. Since it was never put into play it was a failure. But the effort I put into it, as misguided as it was, happened to be the best I could deliver for what I believed was important. In that sense it was an excellent attempt. James's good man would recognize it as that. He would understand that a person's life isn't a scorecard of successes and failures. Rather it's a series of purposes aspired to and the attempts a person makes to fulfill them. Excellence for James's good man is as much about the purpose and the attempt as it is about the actual achievement. For James the social value of the college bred hinged on its commitment to exemplifying and spreading that understanding in the attempt to raise democracy's tone.

Tone? James admits it's a vague word, but from what I can tell it's an attitude a person has about how to conduct her life. The tone that he believed was essential to the health of a democracy ". . . lives by sympathies and admirations, not by dislikes and disdains." College for James is the place where a person can develop those sympathies and admirations. But that's not the end of the story. James believed that the college educated were responsible for spreading this affirming tone throughout society.

"By their tone are all things human either lost or saved. If democracy is to be saved it must catch the higher, healthier tone. If we [the college graduates] are to impress it with our preferences, we ourselves must use the proper tone, which we, in turn, must have caught from our own teachers. It all reverts in the end to the action of innumerable imitative individuals upon each other and to the question of whose tone has the highest spreading power. As a class, we college graduates should look to it that ours has spreading power. It ought to have the highest spreading power."

My reaction? I think James would be disappointed but not surprised by today's college. He would be disappointed because aspiring to know a good man when you see one is not a concern of most students. He would be disappointed because the idea that college graduates should attempt to spread a more uplifting tone throughout society would be rejected by the college bred themselves, on the grounds that it would stand in the way of their pursuit of wealth and power. It would also be condemned by those who never set foot inside academia as nothing more than the manipulation of the public by a privileged clique for the purpose of advancing its self-interest

Disappointed yes, surprised no. Why do I think so? Because James knew that, "There is not a public abuse for which some Harvard advocate may not be found." And he warned, "If a college, through the inferior human influences that have grown regnant there, fails to catch the robuster tone, its failure is colossal, for its social function stops: democracy gives it a wide berth, turns toward it a deaf ear."

Instead of finding college an incubator and laboratory for pursuing excellence in all its diversity, James would discover that it has evolved into a gated community largely inhabited by the driven, the self-involved, and the tone deaf.

29. Occupying Interstices to Raise Democracy's Tone

Dear Emilia,

I think James would react differently towards twentieth century college life. Let's imagine James managed to time travel his way to the present and visit Harvard. Instead of being surprised or disappointed about the tone of the place, I think he'd be intrigued. I make this claim based on the address James gave at Stanford University during the semester he spent there in 1906, "Stanford's Ideal Destiny."

In 1906 Stanford was only fifteen years old and James saw its youth as an advantage. Unlike the universities back east, weighted down with routines and rigidities, Stanford, James observed, had the opportunity to ". . . become something intense and original, not necessarily in point of wealth or extent, but *in point of spiritual quality.*" Another word for the spiritual quality James referred to is tone.

Four years before he wrote "The Social Value of the College Bred," James discussed tone in the address he delivered at Stanford. You defined tone as an attitude that indicates how a person should conduct her life. Given the vagueness of James's description of it in "The Social Value of the College Bred," that isn't far off the mark. In his Stanford address, James more concretely described the spiritual quality that defines tone. First he depicted how it's cultivated within an educational institution. "Like a contagious disease, almost, spiritual life passes from man to man by contact. Education in the long run is an affair that works itself out between the individual student and his opportunities. Methods, of which we talk so much, play but a minor part. Offer the opportunities, leave the student to his natural reaction on them, and he will work out his personal destiny, be it a high one, or a low one. Above all things, offer the opportunity of higher personal contacts. A university provides that anyhow within the student body, for it attracts the more aspiring youth of the country, and they befriend and elevate one another."

He then described the element that gives an institution its tone. "But we are only beginning in this country, with our extraordinary American reliance on organization, to see that the alpha and omega in a university is the *tone* of it, and that this tone is set by human personalities exclusively."

James makes the point that an institution's tone is set by the people within it and not from the organization of the institution itself. I think this is an especially significant distinction to keep in mind for anyone applying to or attending college. The blurring of it contributes to the craziness of the admissions process and the underwhelming reaction many returning seniors have to the first few months of their freshman year. As far as college is concerned a significant number of twenty-first century Americans resemble thirteenth century alchemists. Both believe a common substance can be transmuted into one of greater value by harnessing a magical force. For alchemists the aim was to conjure up the right elixir and turn lead into gold. For meritocrats the goal is to get into the right college and turn a perfectly average student into a star.

Having spent his adult life at Harvard, James wasn't an innocent about the menace that bigness and its offshoot, club opinion had on higher education. Wasn't he sounding the alarm about just that in "The Ph.D. Octopus"? But here's why I think you're wrong about James being disappointed about Harvard's current tone. Experience taught him something young people have yet to learn. Even when the club opinion appears to dominate an institution, there are always persons who will seek out, create, or sustain interstices where they can fashion alternatives to it. James called them the "undisciplinables," those independent thinkers who he believed were Harvard's "proudest product."

I think James would be intrigued rather than disappointed by today's Harvard because he would see more opportunities for her "undisciplinables" to create interstices that undermine the club opinion's hold on the university. These are the opportunities that emerge from the student body's mix of ethnicities, religions, race, and gender orientations. Although far from perfect, Harvard's current attempt at diversity dwarfs anything that was remotely possible in James's day. There are opportunities that emerge from the wide-ranging scope of academic courses offered as well as the clubs, teams, committees, and groups that proliferate on campus. Opportunities emerge from the interactive technologies that mitigate the influence time and space has on communication.

James did more than talk about maintaining interstices of resistance to club opinion; he devoted the last decade of his life to sustaining one. I'm referring to his opposition to the American incursion into the Philippines and his support for anti-imperial and anti-militarist policies. He was mortified by what he considered the perfidy of the McKinley administration. Initially promising to free the Philippines from Spanish rule and to support its independence, the administration reversed itself and authorized American troops to occupy the Philippines and to annex it after the Spanish were expelled. From the history books we know that James's view, supported by the Anti-Imperialist League of which he was an active member, failed to convince enough of the public to denounce McKinley's policies. In an address he delivered to fellow members of the League in 1903, during the last year of the conflict, James admitted as much. "Mr. Chairman: I think we have candidly to admit that in the matter of our Philippine conquest we here and our friends outside have failed to produce much immediate effect. 'Duty and Destiny' have rolled over us like a Juggernaut car whose unwieldy bulk the majority of our countrymen were pushing and pulling forward, and our outcries and attempts to scotch the wheels with our persons haven't acted in the least as a brake."

In your last letter you wrote, "Excellence for James's good man is as much about the purpose and the attempt as it is about the actual achievement. For James the social value of the college bred hinged on its commitment to exemplifying and spreading that understanding in the attempt to raise democracy's tone." That's what James and the League tried to do in mobilizing public opinion against America's occupation of the Philippines. Although the campaign failed on that count, James made the case that it did raise democracy's tone. "Nevertheless, if we look around us today we see a great change from the conditions that prevailed when the outbreak of hostilities first called us into being. Religious emotion and martial hysterics are both over with the public, and the sober fit is on."

The point? You once asked what role an elite played in a democracy. I'd broaden the question to ask, what's the nature of leadership in a democracy? I think it's the ability to create space for individuals of all backgrounds to come together with the purpose of hashing out a higher tone and thinking through how they might spread it. With this in mind I'm making an addition to the syllabus. It's the *Port Huron Statement,* a more recent attempt to raise the tone of American democracy, written by persons not much older than you. I know spring break is coming up and this addition plus James's "The Moral Equivalent of War," isn't exactly the kind of reading a person does on the slopes or by the sea. But I would like you to read the following sections excerpted on *The Sixties Project* website. Go to "Primary Documents and scroll down to "The Port Huron Statement." It's worth digging a little in the site to get a sense of all that was fermenting.

30. On the Outs with the Cancún Contingent

March 13

Dear Doc,

No problem. This senior is not spending spring break near the slopes or the surf. Instead I'll be spending it on Hudson Street. Club opinion around Alden has decided that Emilia Carlyle has forgotten how to have a good time. The perception goes something like this: Anyone foolish enough to include me in her spring break entourage risks spending most of her vacation investigating the lives of the hotel's staff. Consequently, by the time my traveling companion is ready to lay her towel on the beach, she is too guilt ridden to enjoy herself.

If I've learned anything this year it's that shit happens. Apparently an effect my *City as Educator* campaign had was to certify me as too serious, too political, and too intense to kick back. Earlier this semester I got the high school version of the queen bee treatment you experienced in middle school. The difference between the two versions is that the tactics used on me were more subtle than those used on you. I was never publicly humiliated like you were. I was incrementally expunged.

First, some history. As juniors, several of my soccer teammates suggested that we plan to celebrate next year's spring break somewhere warm. By the time we left for summer vacation it was clear that Cancún would be the destination. I started to save money for the trip. Three years ago, my parents made a deal with my sister Kate: she could go to Bermuda for spring break if she paid half. The same deal applied to me.

Fall semester came around and no one, least of all me, was thinking about Cancún. Between the college sweepstakes and the campaign I totally forgot about it. The only time I thought something might be a little weird was right before Christmas vacation. When I was around the girls I was supposed to go with, whether it was in school or out, they never mentioned the trip. I remembered what happened during Christmas vacation when Kate was a senior. She was either on the phone with her friends or they were camped out in her room figuring out what flight to take and what hotel to book. At that point I should have asked what was going on. I didn't pursue it because I was focused on repairing my friendship with Luis.

Suddenly it was the middle of January and I'd heard nothing. So I asked Lilly if she knew anything. Although not a member of the girl's varsity soccer team, Lilly knows everything about social life at Alden. I trust her as a source because she gives it to me straight. Lilly said I had basically been blackballed. My teammates were convinced I had gone over to the dark side by trying to overturn the senior legacy of doing the minimum during second semester. Not one to sugar coat anything, Lilly said many of my teammates believed going with me to Cancún would be about as much fun as having a bikini wax.

I wanted to hear it first-hand. So I confronted Isabelle who was supposed to organize the trip. When I asked her why I was dropped she spun the answer to make it seem as if it was done for my own good. As Isabelle explained it, she and the rest of the girls knew I'd be bored out of my mind spending ten days in Cancún. Furthermore, they knew how much work an independent study with you entailed and figured I'd need spring break just to catch up. At first I was speechless. Then as sarcastically as I could, I thanked Isabelle for looking out for my welfare, and then told her to cut the crap. Only now having gained some distance on the situation can I see how artful her rejection was. I learned something from Isabelle: when those inside the bubble want to expel someone they do it by giving their rejection the appearance of a favor. That way if you fight back you look like an ingrate.

Whether you're a middle-schooler or a graduating senior, being tossed hurts. At home I tried to be as dispassionate about what happened as possible, but that didn't last long. I was just too enraged. After some dinner table venting, my Dad stated the obvious. I had a choice. Either I could be miserable for two weeks wallowing in self-pity and rage, or I could use the two weeks to explore one of the world's greatest cities.

Two weeks—for once in my life I'd have the time to take on NYC. Dad suggested I get a copy of *Time Out* and plan my "staycation."

Well, I bought *Time Out* and am planning what exhibits to go to, movies to see, maybe take in a play. Luis's vacation overlaps with mine for a few days, so we'll probably do something together. Also not every Alden student goes to Vail or Cancún. There are kids around. But it's funny. Last year a lot of what I did was determined by who I did it with, this year not so much. I'm getting comfortable having myself as company, and am beginning to understand the difference between loneliness and solitude. It comes down to purpose. Knowing why you want to do something is the best defense against loneliness, even if you do it by yourself. One of my purposes this vacation is to take the *Port Huron Statement* and do something I've never done before—read it in the Rose Reading Room of the NYPL.

PS If I write anything over the break can I send it to you?

31. Doc Makes the Case for Solitude

Dear Emilia

Yes, knowing your purpose does contribute to the distinction between loneliness and solitude, but I think it goes deeper than that. At bottom I see the difference as a consequence of the relationship a person has with her inner life. A solitary person is with herself. A lonely person is without others. To be with oneself is the outcome of learning to trust one's inner dialogue. That trust is built up over the years as a person attempts to discover her purposes and establish an autonomous self. Her inner voices—whether decisive, skeptical, argumentative, cautionary, recriminating, imaginative, comforting, judgmental, or ironic—become familiar and sought after companions.

Unlike solitude, loneliness is predicated on a lack of trust for one's inner life. Having never seriously thought about her purposes, the conversation a lonely person has with herself is like a set of recordings cobbled together from received opinions, societal imperatives, manufactured tastes and desires. Because a lonely person's inner life is basically filled with communiqués and dispatches from the outside, the most terrifying condition for her to endure is to be without others. In that state her inner voice becomes inaudible and the sense of who she is vanishes. Even though a lonely person desperately needs others to provide her with a sense of self, loneliness causes a person to isolate herself from the world. The irony is that a solitary person, who has cultivated an autonomous sense of self and therefore doesn't depend on others to define who she is, seeks connections with the world.

Among the reasons a person seeks out solitude is to hear herself think and to get a different perspective on her circumstances. Just imagine the stock image of someone immersed in solitude. There would be a lone figure situated in a sublime natural setting usually by an ocean and/or mountain, gazing out towards the horizon, ostensibly wondering what her place in the universe is.

This image depicts solitude as a condition that makes it possible for us to engage in a different kind of knowing, different from the mental effort we usually associate with gaining knowledge. That effort, dedicated to shaping the world according to our will, is characterized by abstracting, searching, concluding, analyzing, deducing, proving, testing, and comparing. The knowing associated with solitude is receptive. Reason holds the will in abeyance so we can observe, contemplate, comprehend, meditate, study the world as is, and connect with what is hidden and silenced by the demands of daily life.

For me the best location for listening and observing the world isn't bucolic but urban. Call it perverse, but a city street or enclave is where I find the solitude and the receptivity it engenders. Perverse? Think city street—crowds, every type of sensory distraction known to humankind, and the need to think of nothing else but where you're going—comes to mind. That's an accurate portrayal of street life, but it's not the whole story. More often than not, I'll be walking down a street when something—it could be as mundane as a newly planted window box—catches my eye. That window box filled with flowers concentrates my power of observation: I notice the different varieties. It activates my sense of wonder: who took time to do this? It even connects me to something beyond myself: finally spring has arrived.

At least I'm in good company when it comes to thinking of the city as an environment hospitable to solitude. Charles Baudelaire, Walter Benjamin, Alfred Kazin each wrote about his experiences as a solitary walker in the city. Reading and rereading their work, I'm always struck at how essential mastering the art of paying attention is to becoming a walker in the city. Paying attention for them doesn't have its usual connotation of narrowing one's focus, staying on task, keeping one's sight set on a particular goal. Rather, paying attention for these solitary walkers broadens and deepens their focus. They listen to silences, they find what is lost, they search for the mystery housed within the mundane, and they uncover deeply hidden relations among superficial differences. It's this form of paying attention, a collecting of impressions and appreciations that nourishes the inner life.

Paying attention to one's surroundings has been on my mind lately. It's an essential skill for next year's *City as Educator* course. I've come up with some exercises I hope will sharpen students' powers of observation. I've attached a copy of them.

I'm also going to ask students taking the course to find a place that offers them some solitude in the city. Recently, I passed one of my favorite locations. It's the statue of Eleanor Roosevelt on Seventy-second Street and Riverside Drive. However frenzied the day, if I can eke out some time to spend in her company, I can usually regain some perspective on what matters. I simply sit down on a bench, stare at the statue, and ask myself, what would Eleanor think?

And yes, I will be reading my email during the break.

32. Conversation about a Community Activist and Other Dinner Party Illuminations

March 26

Dear Doc,

I can't believe the vacation is half over. At the beginning I thought the two weeks would be the worst, but they turned out better than I anticipated, mainly because I've been spending time "observing my neighborhood." No I haven't been practicing your attention exercises, but my neighborhood was the center of attention last weekend.

On Saturday my parents hosted their annual dinner for professional colleagues and friends. Since my sophomore year I've attended this event initially because Luis would be there, but also to listen to the conversation and observe my parents interact with their peers. Watching them, I've come to realize that they have professional expertise and knowledge that predates my arrival and is distinct from what they know and do as parents. It's a powerful realization second only to the one I had in middle school when suddenly out of nowhere I realized, "Oh my god, my parents must have had sex; otherwise my sister and I wouldn't be here!"

Anyway this year's dinner was particularly interesting. Most of the conversation centered on the controversy I told you about—the one over NYU's expansion plans. Last month my father went to the meeting where Community Board 2 unanimously rejected the university's plan. I figured that meant the fight was over and the community won: NYU would have to expand somewhere else, probably in Brooklyn. But everyone else at the dinner, including Luis, didn't see it that way. They thought NYU would modify some of the plan's features to meet the demands of the city's planning commission. And in the summer, when the Council votes, the plan would be approved.

The conversation took off from there. My father's partner asked, "How would Jane Jacobs handle this? The overriding issue hasn't changed since she battled Robert Moses to save Washington Square Park. It remains a question of who should have the authority to determine what gets built in a neighborhood—the people who actually live there or the planners, politicians, architects and developers." Not only didn't I know who Jane Jacobs and Robert Moses were, but also it was news to me that the park I've considered my personal playground was threatened not so long ago.

A friend of my mother's replied that she didn't think Jacob's grass roots organizing would work in this situation because NYU is embedded in the community and a much smoother adversary than Moses. Lena said, "Whereas Moses actually called Jane and her supporters 'stupid and selfish,' Alicia Hurley, the Vice President for Government and Civic Engagement, constantly emphasizes how much the university appreciates the community's input. Whether that input makes any difference isn't the point. Even the charade of community outreach goes a long way to co-opt opposition."

There was more discussion about the features the community found objectionable in NYU's plan and how the university could scale it back while still getting the space it needed. Then someone I didn't recognize made a comment. He said, "Basically the utopian vision that characterized the sixties was furthered by the work of three women writers: Jane Jacobs, Betty Friedan, and Rachel Carson." Betty Friedan I knew something about, but the others meant nothing to me. I asked Luis if he knew anything about Robert Moses, Jane Jacobs, or Rachel Carson. He was as clueless as I was. After everyone left we bombarded my parents with questions about who these people were and why they remain famous.

The post dinner Q and A session motivated me to organize my summer reading list: *The Power Broker*, *Death and Life of Great American Cities*, *Silent Spring*, and *The Feminine Mystique* should keep me busy. I think Luis might also read *The Power Broker*. He was particularly interested in Moses after my father described the lengths Moses went to remove the East Tremont Community because it was blocking the construction of the Cross Bronx Expressway. I also learned that Jane Jacobs lived a few blocks from us at 555 Hudson Street. At some point I want to go to the New York Historical Society and find photographs that show what my street looked like when she lived here.

I have more to tell about the dinner and reading the *Port Huron Statement,* but Lilly has appeared and we have tickets for the movies. It feels great to be going out on a Monday night.

33. Emilia Voices Reservations about Utopian Visions

Dear Doc,

The last email left off just as I was going to tell you how the dinner party my parents gave helped me put the *Port Huron Statement* into perspective. It was the mystery guest's description of the sixties as a decade of utopian vision that did it. My gut reaction after reading the sections you assigned was, it all sounds terrific but what good are ideals that never become real? Fifty years later I'm left wondering whether utopian thinking serves any purpose. Now, instead of the mixed income neighborhoods Jane Jacobs advocated we have gated cities, instead of Betty Friedan's dream of gender equality, feminism is my generation's "f" word. Rachel Carson won the DDT fight, but currently more eco systems are under siege from threats she never envisioned. As for the *Port Huron Statement's* participatory democracy, I'd say the Occupy Movement is its latest incarnation. But for all the publicity about the 99 percent, it doesn't even have the clout to bring members of the one percent who aided and abetted the financial crisis to trial.

I wasn't surprised by the utopian vision of the *Port Huron Statement*. I imagine that the Civil Rights movement allowed college students to believe anything was possible. The Vietnam War and the draft made peace and disarmament literally a matter of life and death for them and participatory democracy a means for not ending up in a body bag.

Finding a way to eliminate war was also the foundation of James's utopian vision. But his vision differed from the one described by the writers of the *Port Huron Statement*. Unlike them, James didn't reject military values per se; he argued they had to be redirected. My guess is that by the time the student activists met in Port Huron, the military had grown so big, in the Jamesian sense, that redirecting its values towards goals other than winning wars was impossible.

On first reading "The Moral Equivalent of War," it appeared as if James was contradicting himself. His support of "martial virtues" like ". . . intrepidity, contempt of softness, surrender of private interest, obedience to command . . ." was exactly what a person who wanted to outlaw war wouldn't do. James' made his hatred of war explicit when he "confessed" his utopia: "I devoutly believe in the reign of peace and in the gradual advent of some sort of a socialistic equilibrium. The fatalistic view of the war-function is to me nonsense, for I know that war-making is due to definite motives and subject to prudential checks and reasonable criticisms, just like any other form of enterprise. And when whole nations are the armies, and the science of destruction vies in intellectual refinement with the sciences of production, I see that war becomes absurd and impossible from its own monstrosity. Extravagant ambitions will have to be replaced by reasonable claims, and nations must take common cause against them. I see no reason why all this should not apply to yellow as well as white countries, and I look forward to a future when acts of war shall be formally outlawed as between civilized peoples."

All of this begs the question: How is James going to bring this off? The short version—by connecting the martial values he acknowledged and the utopian vision he desired to make real. James believed peace would never be preserved until it offers a moral equivalent to war. For him that required a vision that would enable a community to use the martial virtues as means to serve peaceful ends. His plan for bringing that about called for replacing the military draft with ". . . a conscription of the whole youthful population to form for a certain number of years a part of the army enlisted against *Nature*."

Talk about politically incorrect, hasn't the whole environmental movement been about conserving, sustaining, and restoring nature? However as I continued to read, I began to realize that James's battle against nature had nothing to do with picking off buffalo from a train going cross country or going on safari to kill as many exotic animals as possible. Rather it's what we would call building infrastructure.

James argued that this type of conscription would serve two purposes. It would improve the standard of living for the many and eradicate the club opinion of the few. "The military ideals of hardihood and discipline would be wrought into the growing fibre of the people; no one would remain blind as the luxurious classes now are blind, to man's real relations to the globe he lives on, and to the permanently sour and hard foundations of his higher life. To coal and iron mines, to freight trains, to fishing fleets in December, to dishwashing, clothes-washing, and window-washing, to road-building and tunnel-making, to foundries and stoke-holes, and to the frames of skyscrapers, would our gilded youths be drafted off, according to their choice, to get the childishness knocked out of them, and to come back into society with healthier sympathies and soberer ideas."

The idea I took away from reading "The Moral Equivalent of War" was that for peace to prevail a society needs an aspiration that mobilizes its collective will like war has throughout history. In particular young people need something of heroic proportions to activate their moral compass and for James that doesn't mean becoming a first class consumer. I think he's right about the young, but James's utopian vision needs to be updated if it's to carry any weight in the present.

Instead of battling nature, how about drafting the world's youth into Mother Nature's Army. Instead of fighting each other, these recruits would fight against the effects of global warming in their neighborhoods. They could build green infrastructure, everything from bicycle lanes to high speed rails, save endangered species, bank seeds, clean up polluted sites, plant trees and gardens, practice sustainable agriculture, generally doing what is needed to green the planet. I think altering James's utopian vision would give the slogan think globally act locally credibility. Will it happen? Considering that in this country we're still debating whether climate change is real or not, I seriously doubt it.

Finally, my grandparents came over the other day and asked what I was up to aside from waiting to hear from colleges. I told them about reading James's essays and how I was particularly interested in his idea of tone and his insistence that "... by their tone all things human are either lost or saved." I also told them that I was reading the *Port Huron Statement* and found it utopian to the point of being a fairy tale.

Well, both of my grandparents who were college students in the early sixties didn't see it that way. They made it clear that back in the day the *Port Huron Statement* was considered a manifesto. As my grandfather said, "It summoned us to change the world and assured us we could do it." He asked me how I would characterize the present tone and I replied, "anxious." How could it be otherwise when all that can be expected from the current crop of world leaders is stale solutions to unprecedented problems? Even in a school like Alden whose students are largely shielded from economic insecurities, the future seems filled with hazards. The worry is if some climatic "event" doesn't upend it, a kid from Shanghai with the smarts and the skills will.

34. 'Having It All' and Russian Roulette

Dear Emilia,

I've spent a few days unplugged and only now have read your last two emails. It sounds like your staycation surpassed all expectations. Discovering Robert Moses, Jane Jacobs, and Rachel Carson isn't too shabby a way to spend a two-week break. As for the summer, I think you'll find that reading about the battle between Moses and Jacobs presents the urban version of the David and Goliath story, as well as depicting two distinctly different interpretations of power.

Owing to your newfound interest, you might check out Jane's Walk NYC (go to site of the Municipal Art Society of New York, mas.org, and look under "programs"). To honor Jane Jacobs, MAS will host nearly seventy free walking tours throughout the city on May 5th and 6th. Persons who actually live in the neighborhoods conduct the tours. That's the part that really honors Jacobs's spirit since she believed residents have the most intimate knowledge of where they live.

Your question about whether a utopian vision serves any purpose is extremely important. Fortunately during these last days of the break, I have the leisure to respond thoughtfully. I'd argue it does, when used as a means to activate a society's sense of possibility. That being said, it's apparent that you're ambivalent about its effects. On one hand you criticize the *Port Huron Statement* as utopian to the point of being a fairy tale. On the other, you create a twenty first century utopian vision—Mother Nature's Youthful Army. My guess is that your ambivalence is a consequence of equating a society's sense of possibility with a blue print for the total realization of potentials.

How does a utopian vision activate a society's sense of possibility? It's relatively straightforward: if you can't imagine anything other than what is, nothing will change. A utopian vision activates a society's sense of possibility by throwing into relief what is skewed, insane, cruel, and dehumanizing about our daily lives. It illuminates the ways in which we have become complicit in and accustomed to the absurdities and lies that are regarded as normal.

I think this is what the authors of the *Port Huron Statement* did well, especially in explaining the conditions that moved them and their generation from complacency to activism. "With nuclear energy whole cities can easily be powered, yet the dominant nation-states seem more likely to unleash destruction greater than that incurred in all wars of human history. Although our own technology is destroying old and creating new forms of social organization, men still tolerate meaningless work and idleness."

A utopian vision as a blueprint for the total realization of potentials might generate awe but not a sense of possibility. Humans are finite and mortal. Totality, having it all, demands a level of control over circumstances and timelessness that is godlike not human. When a utopian vision is understood by a society to be a blueprint for the total realization of its potentials the consequences are dire.

One effect is cultural despair. Since total realization is an illusion, over time, the accumulation of ill-fated attempts to achieve it engenders a deep-seated cynicism. Ultimately nothing becomes worth the effort. You are left with a society in which any aspiration is disparaged; you are left with a society without hope.

The other effect of interpreting a utopian vision as a blueprint for total realization of potentials is the perversion of reality. To make people believe in an illusion, imperfect, incomplete realities have to be eradicated from a society's consciousness and replaced by a system of lies. That system is called an ideology. One of the best descriptions I've read about how an ideology works is by Vaclav Havel in "The Power of the Powerless."

An ideology must convince people that the illusion it

serves " . . . is in harmony with the human order and the order of the universe." To bring this about an ideology creates" . . . a world of appearances trying to pass for reality." In order to survive, even persons who don't believe the lies must behave as though they do. "They need not accept the lie. It is enough for them to have accepted their life with it and in it. For this very fact, individuals confirm the system, fulfill the system, make the system, are the system." Remember the story about the emperor who went around butt naked but everyone acted as if he was clothed? That's the storybook example of an ideology at work.

On the personal level visions of utopia are ideals. Like their social counterpart ideals can lead either to a compulsion to have it all or to an urge to achieve meaningful fulfillment. For most of history the individual effort to have it all was considered a grievous transgression. The classical world called it hubris; the Judeo-Christian called it the sin of pride. In both cases a human being violated the natural order, the limits of mortality, for he believed himself to be godlike.

Let's be clear. Having it all is different from the pursuit of excellence. The latter is grounded in actual human accomplishments, not some abstract notion of superiority. Excellence, whether it manifests itself as Olympic gold, a standing ovation, the Nobel Prize, or a four star restaurant invigorates a person's sense of reality rather than twisting it as a false sense of superiority over others.

Whereas the pursuit of having it all creates a cadre of the select, alienating one person from another, the pursuit of excellence emboldens our shared humanity because it enriches the sense of possibility for all. Take for example the dance performance I saw recently. As much as I love the dance, I know regardless of how much I would have dedicated myself to it, I'd never be more than mediocre. But watching the dancers on stage move with the grace and the precision that has always eluded me, I don't feel diminished but joyous. There on stage is one of my own, who is actually defying gravity.

Unlike the reach for superiority, striving for excellence

isn't at odds with embracing an ideal that makes fulfillment possible for all. Both excellence and fulfillment emerge from the lived circumstances of one's life. To achieve either or both a person needs to judge what is meaningful not according to a set of external criteria but according to the priorities she sets for herself. Both fulfillment and excellence require a person to trust her inner voice, have confidence in her capacity to judge soundly even while conscious of the possibility for error, to learn from her mistakes, and to carry on.

In my opinion what is particularly dangerous about growing up in a society like ours is that a young person is led to believe that achieving the possibility of fulfillment and having it all is one and the same thing. Today, instead of being considered a transgression, the pursuit of superiority, having it all, is considered a virtue—leading to success and happiness and not insignificantly to a robust economy. A respect for limits is considered a sin or at least heretical, even though limits are essential for achieving a sense of fulfillment.

In twenty-first century America, to proclaim something is enough is to spout a defeatist doctrine. Nothing is ever enough in a winner-take-all society. Either you're in the game driven by the ideology of winner-take-all, or you're out of the game, a born loser. And as with all ideologies, one must never question whether the game is worth playing and whether the goal you are driven to attain is real.

As I'm writing about the personal costs exacted by the winner-take-all culture, I find myself thinking about Caleb and the other students I've known over the years who have taken their own lives. What strikes me is how similar the initial reactions to these tragedies were: shock, grief, and finally utter bewilderment. How could someone so gifted, who had everything to live for, do this? I wouldn't presume to know the answer for each death, but I suspect one constant that made the unthinkable actual was a lethal confusion.

The confusion was about the difference between achieving personal fulfillment and gaining public superiority. The confusion that killed was about which of these ends were worth a person's commitment. To state the obvious, the social pressure to win public superiority is overwhelming. And even if these young people recognized that such superiority was a mirage, they probably felt helpless when it came to deciding to stop chasing it. So they cleared the hurdles, gathered the prizes, attained the successes, all the time goaded by a sense of emptiness that inevitably leads to an overwhelming feeling of entrapment—offering no exit except death. As a society we protect adolescents from a whole host of threats—everything from drunk drivers, STDS, drugs, even wayward peanuts in the cafeteria—but when it comes to the winner-take-all ideology, we allow our youth to play Russian roulette. Isn't that the height of insanity?

To be continued when we meet next Monday.

35. Crossing a Finish Line

Dear Doc,

Harvard accepted me and I accepted it. To its credit Harvard has already changed my life. Being accepted has done wonders for my social status around school. The character flaws that made me *persona non grata* with the Cancún contingent—too serious, too intense, too weird—have magically been transformed into quirky but endearing qualities.

After Luis congratulated me, he asked if I would hold a séance to contact James. That way James could act as my personal college guide. I told Luis it was the other way around. Since James was the one with the mystical know how, he has contacted me and together we've planned his return to the Yard.

Luis also has reason to celebrate. He got into Cornell and Cooper Union. He's going to Cornell. Between the Cornell grant he was awarded and the federal work-study program he's been accepted to, he'll be able to graduate debt free. I told you he was worried about moving out of the city because it would leave his mother with no one to help at home. Luis finally talked to her about it and she told him she'd manage. Over the summer her youngest sister is going to move in and take up the slack. Mercedes has a part time job in a beauty salon near Luis's apartment and she'll continue attending Bronx Community College. Now the only question is whether this boy, born and raised in the Bronx, will be able to endure so much nature and a winter that can start in October and last until May.

As for Lilly, who was accepted early to Harvard, she was pleased that I was accepted. To know Lilly is to know she doesn't get excited. Immediately after telling me how pleased she was, she made it clear that becoming roommates isn't going to happen. I couldn't agree more. Lilly also let me know that if she spots any sign of my wanting to organize the Harvard student body into missionaries promoting social uplift she will immediately call the appropriate authorities.

To celebrate, the three of us are going on several of the Jacobs walks. Lilly has known Luis for as long as I have and they are good friends, although to be around the two of them when they're together you'd wouldn't think so. Each derives pleasure from annoying the other. For instance when I asked if they wanted to go on the walk, Lilly announced that since she will soon be taking up residence in Cambridge she should visit the provinces. In Lilly's world that means going to the outer boroughs. Not missing a beat Luis replied, that since she's a citizen of the land of limitless trust funds, she'd need a visa. It should prove to be an interesting weekend.

For my part, I'm glad it's Harvard. One of the unexpected effects of reading James is I've developed an interest in the place as an institution. There's nothing like studying the past to convince you that nothing is perfect, even Harvard. I've often wondered what James would think if, like Luis suggested, he could cross over for a return engagement to his Alma Mater. Short of that I'll have to settle for reading his *Talks To Students*.

36. Emilia Finds Some Words

April 26

Dear Doc,

It took less than a month for the euphoria of getting into Harvard to turn into anxiety about going there. Actually that's not quite accurate. Even when I, and everyone around me, was thrilled, pleased, excited, relieved, or overjoyed about my being accepted, I felt the beginnings of a knot forming in my stomach. The trouble was until a few days ago I couldn't figure out why.

My nervousness made no sense. I'm going to the university that's my first choice. The standard freshman worries—inability to keep up academically, fear of not fitting in—don't bother me. I know I can handle all of that, and if not, I'll be able to find someone who can help.

Then around three in the morning it came to me. Come September, I'll be entering the belly of the beast as far as the ideology of perfection is concerned. At a school like Harvard it's just so easy to believe the illusion of perfection is real. How could it not be? Obviously anyone selected to join this community has been defying limits all her life. So why stop now? There's no better setting than Harvard to continue demonstrating how close to perfect you are.

One thought led to another until I realized I'm at a crossroads largely because of what I've come to understand from writing these letters: I'm responsible for educating myself. If I buy into the ideology of perfection I give up that responsibility and Harvard will become Alden on steroids. Given that, how can I be sure I'll assume the responsibility for my education? To put it in more concrete terms: How do I know that as an undergraduate I won't end up clearing the hurdles like I did in high school? How do I know I'll be able to distinguish between success and fulfillment, perfection and excellence? How do I know I'll have the courage to listen to my inner voice when it opposes the club opinion?

I turned to "Talks To Students" looking for assurance that to know what's right will inevitably lead to doing it. Not surprisingly James didn't deliver on that. In fact he asserted that doubt is the origin of a person's education. "Doubt itself is an active state. The radical sign of will, the essential mark of that achieved development which makes man capable of speculating on all things and raises him to his dignity of an independent and autonomous being, is the possibility of doubt."

For James living with doubt is essential for raising a person's tone, putting forth her best effort, building character. "Not a victory is gained, not a deed of faithfulness or courage is done, except upon a maybe; not a service, not a sally of generosity, not a scientific exploration or experiment or textbook, that may not be a mistake. It is only by risking our persons from one hour to another that we live at all. It is all a question of maybe."

I must have read these lines ten times. They rocked my world. Until then I thought doubt was a condition to be avoided. Wasn't the purpose of schooling to end or at least lessen it? There's no room for doubt when I'm filling in some standardized test's bubble sheet or taking a multiple-choice test. I've yet to hand in a lab report that concluded with, "I'm not sure." Even the history and English essays I've written always come down on one side of an argument or another.

Doc, I got these quotes from reading Richardson's biography of James and not "Talks To Students". I decided not to finish "Talks" because much of what was in it we already discussed. I wanted to read the biography because I needed to find out what role doubt played in James's life, especially when he was young. No exaggeration, his early life was filled with it to the point of causing him to doubt who he was. At twenty-eight James's lack of self-confidence caused him to suffer a nervous breakdown. He described the terror that overcame him by using the cover of a letter written by a French correspondent and sent to him.

"Whilst in this state of philosophic pessimism and general

depression of spirits about my prospects, I went one evening in a dressing-room in the twilight to procure some article that was there: when suddenly there fell upon me without warning, just as if it came out of the darkness, a horrible fear of my own existence. Simultaneously there arose in my mind the image of an epileptic patient whom I had seen in the asylum, a black-haired youth with greenish skin, entirely idiotic, who used to sit all day on one of the benches, or rather shelves against the wall, with his knees drawn up against his chin, and the coarse grey undershirt, which was the only garment, drawn over him enclosing his entire figure . . . . This image and my fear entered into a species of combination with each other. That shape am I, I felt, potentially. Nothing that I possess can defend me against that fate, if the hour for it should strike for me as it struck for him."

How do you recover from a nervous breakdown before Prozac? If you're William James you read and think yourself towards recovery: Maybe today we'd call that cognitive therapy. James read the work of the French philosopher, Charles Renouvier, during his convalescence and conceived an idea that saved him: He wrote in his diary, "I think that yesterday was a crisis in my life. I finished the first part of Renouvier's 2nd Essay and saw no reason why his definition of free will—the sustaining of a thought because I choose to when I might have other thoughts—need be the definition of an illusion. At any rate, I will—assume for the present—until next year—that it is no illusion. My first act of free will shall be to believe in free will." James's yearlong experiment would become the guiding principle for the rest of his life.

Without knowing it James's idea about free will was what I needed to hear. It helped me understand something that on one level is simple but on another profound. Harvard isn't going to make me clear the hurdles or live inside the bubble; I will choose to or not. James's decision to believe in free will answered a question that I realized was at the root of my nervousness: What can you know when you accept that there is no certainty? You know you are free to choose one idea over another and act on it.

James puts it this way, "'*Will you or won't you have it so?*' is the most probing question we are ever asked; we are asked it every hour of the day, and about the largest as well as the smallest, the most theoretical as well as the most practical, things . . . . We answer by consents or non-consents and not by words. What wonder that these dumb responses should seem our deepest organs of communication with the nature of things! What wonder if the effort demanded by them be the measure of our worth as men! What wonder if the amount which we accord of it be the one strictly underived and original contribution which we make to the world!"

From all of this I understand that I was asking myself the wrong question. The question isn't—can I take responsibility for my own education? The question is—will I? Whether the outcome is a success or failure isn't what's important. There's no way I can know that until I decide to act. What matters is to decide to choose and give it my best shot. That's the freedom worthy of a liberal arts education.

Which brings me to Caleb. Ever since he died, I've been wondering if there wasn't something I could have said to prevent it. If I had the words back then I would have told Caleb that doubt is not bad, and being lost because of it isn't permanent. I'd tell him that doubt makes a person aware that there are ways of living other than the one that is making him miserable. I'd tell Caleb that the only thing anyone can know for sure is that life is lived according to maybe, and instead of that being terrifying it can be a source of comfort, strength and freedom. Once a person gives up the quest for certainty the question is no longer—can I do something? Rather it becomes—will I do it? Making that choice is to choose to set oneself free. What can I say Doc? I regret not having those words months ago.

I don't want to end this letter with a regret but with a question. Do you remember Luis's smart-ass idea about my channeling James and taking him with me to Harvard? No, I'm not inviting you to a séance as my end of school project. But his suggestion brings back a memory. As a preschooler I had two imaginary friends Jake-ee and Moomer. I remember consulting them whenever I needed to make a choice and wasn't sure what to do. Each morning I'd ask them to help me choose my clothes for the day. Looking at some photos from those years, I'm surprised my mother let me out in public. I'm older, but I have to admit, I'd like nothing better than to have Professor James drop by my dorm room for a chat. Does a person ever outgrow the need for an imaginary friend to help her work through the doubt?

37. Finding Intimations of the Possible in a Well-Formed Ankle and a Polka-Dotted Cravat

May 1

Dear Emilia,

No, I don't think anyone outgrows the need to consult with her imaginary friends, and I speak from personal experience. At bottom, whether the conversation is with Jake-ee, Moomer, William, or Eleanor isn't it actually the continuous discussion a person has with herself about what matters? Sitting and gazing at Eleanor's statue my mind "unclamps" as James described it in *Talks To Students,* and the associations it makes are " . . . copious, and varied, and effective."

But I have to tell you Emilia, what delights me the most when I visit Eleanor are her ankles. Petite, graceful, feminine, I imagine them ensconced in ladylike pumps supporting her as she greets coal miners in Appalachia, supports Marian Anderson, resists her mother-in-law, drafts the Universal Declaration of Human Rights, and claims her space amidst Washington's cigars and pin stripes.

As for transporting an effigy of William James to Cambridge I wouldn't worry about it. Harvard has it covered. Try to find some time during the frenzy of orientation week to visit Room 107 in Emerson Hall. That's where the philosophy department is located. Hanging on the wall you'll spot a portrait of Professor James. For a preview, google "William James portrait Harvard", then download the PDF of "The Bechtel Room: A Guide to the Portraits."

If you haven't guessed by now, he along with Eleanor is another of my heroes. I think of James as my intellectual trainer. After reading him I feel as if my mind has undergone a rigorous workout, revitalizing interpretations of familiar questions and boosting my confidence to explore new ones. Like a good session in the gym, time spent in James's company increases my zest quotient.

I feel about James the way you feel about Bourne. I struggled with James and through it he became for me a reference point in seeking to craft a well-made self. By well made, I mean a self that uses what a person knows, as grounding for who she is, and how she acts. A self, in other words, that exemplifies integrity; William James is one of my exemplars of integrity.

I trust James as a thinker and a writer because I trust James as a man. From reading his letters and several biographies, I've come to think of him as waging a constant inner struggle to achieve the unity between thought, feeling, and action he championed in his work. As his reader, I am struck by James's personal struggle to live his principles and to generate principles that live.

Reading him gives me a sense of clarity and companionship. James is one of my heroes because I admire what he does with his protean critical intelligence. In my view, he uses it to unmask and to resist cynicism, an especially pernicious vice because it disguises personal and cultural defeatism as sophisticated thought and cultivated feeling. James is my hero because his words help me recognize cynicism when I see it and prevent it from corrupting my spirit.

For my taste, the James represented in the portrait looks too unapproachable. From the photographs I've seen, I imagine James as a less austere and commanding presence, a man, who in spite of knowing the abyss, still managed to embrace the life around him. Although I don't think the painting brings that across, a sentence in the entry that accompanies it does. "James was a colorful character in the Department, sometimes wearing polka-dot cravats at a time when only 'Bohemians,' radicals, and the avant-garde wore such flashy dress, and teaching his course in his parlor wearing only pants, suspenders, and an undershirt."

Why am I fixated on Eleanor's ankles and William's polka-dot cravat? They recommend a world replete with incongruities, improbabilities, surprises, and possibilities which each of us can choose to incorporate into our life's story. If you choose to do so Emilia, such an undertaking will require your best effort and will ultimately form you into the person you aspire to be.

Afterword

Having accompanied Emilia on her senior year odyssey, we, like her, face a couple of unknowns. Although Emilia has come to recognize that she is responsible for her education, whether she puts that recognition into practice during her college years is not certain. Equally uncertain is whether Emilia's growing awareness of the inequalities that pervade her world will have an impact on her sense of purpose. As Doc knows and James wrote, once Emilia graduates from Alden it is "... all a question of maybe."

Whereas the qualities that will shape Emilia's character over the next four years are unknown, the qualities that shape Alden's tone are apparent. In the course of their correspondence, Doc and Emilia provide us with glimpses of the persons, routines, resources, and expectations that characterize their school. James observed that an educational institution's tone emerged from "...the action of innumerable imitative individuals upon each other." With so much talk about the need to improve American schooling, I would like to examine how excellence emerges from the imitative action that takes place in a school like Alden.

It starts with a recognition shared among the school's constituencies. At Alden, students are perceived as persons capable of and responsible for shaping their purposes, rather than as members of a cohort destined to fulfill a variety of abstract and predetermined ends. Alden puts that recognition into practice by instituting policies that cultivate its students' mixture of interests and talents. Class size is the most obvious means of doing so. Classes at Alden top out at eighteen—a number that makes possible the give and take of a pedagogy based on the seminar. With classes capped at eighteen, students understand that more is expected of them than just showing up. Instead, each member of the class is expected to contribute by listening, commenting, raising and answering questions.

Small classes also influence a teacher's choice of assignments. One of the indicators of an excellent school is its ability to graduate students who can write well. Whether it's writing an analytical essay for history, a short story for English, or a lab report for physics, students become skilled through regular practice that occurs across the curriculum. In no small part the amount of written work assigned at a school is a consequence of class size. Still the impact class size has on the quality of instruction remains controversial. The research is neither definitive nor effective because the suggested reduction in student numbers doesn't get below the threshold at which a writing intensive pedagogy becomes feasible. A history teacher who teaches four sections with eighteen students in each is more likely to assign an essay as a means of evaluation than a colleague teaching five sections with thirty. Finding himself responsible for grading 150 essays and for returning them in a timely fashion, even a teacher dedicated to incorporating more writing in his instruction would be hard pressed not to hear the siren song of short answer testing.

But simply assigning more writing assignments does not a writer make. Time is needed—time for the teacher to read and comment on what the student has submitted, time for both to go over the comments, and time for the student to make revisions. Although time is highly structured at Alden, free time is built into the day making possible the one-on-one meetings these tasks require. Because these meetings provide opportunities for a teacher and a student to interact outside of the classroom, it's not uncommon, in the course of going over an assignment, for a student to bring up some personal concern or goal. Over time, these "tangential" conversations often deepen the perception a student and her teacher have of one another.

Another policy that affirms Alden's recognition of its students as persons capable of and responsible for shaping their purposes is its commitment to offering an expansive curriculum. Alden's list of course offerings literally spans the millenniums—from Latin and ancient Greek to computer science.

The wide-ranging scope of Alden's curriculum is largely due to how its constituencies interpret the purpose of K-12 instruction. As they see it, a K-12 school is responsible for introducing a student to as many different ways of knowing about the world as it can. Since the interests and capabilities of children and adolescents are rarely apparent and certainly not fixed, it's essential that a K-12 school offer a rich array of subjects so that its students will be better equipped to discover what their interests and capabilities are. That's why in a school like Alden, one doesn't hear talk about art as a frill, getting back to basics, or what subjects to cut because only a handful of students are enrolled.

Even with all of these policies in place, Alden can't guarantee every student will flourish. Caleb's suicide alerts us to the reality that privilege alone is not a foolproof prophylactic against boredom, mediocrity, and self-destructive behaviors. Still, given that reality, no voice at Alden is raised in defense of increasing class size, doing away with free time, or limiting the curriculum's scope for the sake of cost effectiveness. In schools like Alden, small classes, free time, and an expansive curriculum don't provoke controversy because they're perceived as the necessary material conditions for making excellence possible. But that's not the whole story. For excellence to take root at Alden, or any other school, the tone that should pervade its halls is one of trust—trust that members of its community are capable of seeing each another as persons.

How does that come about? Whether trust takes hold or not in a school community is a consequence of the quality of the relationships formed within it. As much as K-12 education is about skill development and learning content, it's also about students trying to piece together who they want to become. They do this by discovering glimpses of their future selves in their peers and adults. The adults students choose to trust are those they recognize as having gone through the same process they are undergoing—trying to figure out what matters and to form themselves accordingly.

A school like Alden makes time for this type of recognition.

Along with one-on-one conversations, there are assemblies where teachers can demonstrate their passion for something other than their subject matter. Some teachers give a concert or a dramatic reading. Others talk about a recent trip they've taken, an issue they're passionate about, or a project they're working on.

As important as these planned activities are for allowing students to see their teachers as engaged and multi-faceted adults, equally important are the serendipitous encounters that occur in schools like Alden. Those encounters occur in the interstices of the school day—whenever and wherever Alden students congregate and socialize. Whether in the hallways between classes, before and after school, in the cafeteria during lunch or just hanging out during free periods, these times offer Alden's students and teachers a chance to experience one another as persons rather than as individuals defined by their roles. Serendipitous encounters are particularly powerful because a student may walk away having gotten a sense of a well-made self. A self that "... is an ordered set of reflections, conclusions, and convictions."[3]

Serendipity struck my department one Friday afternoon during, the "end of week wrap-up." The wrap-up started as an impromptu conversation giving my colleagues and me the opportunity to talk to one another as fellow historians. We would discuss the news of the day and often how it relates to a variety of historical themes. In addition, we would trade opinions about current books, movies, or museum exhibitions particularly noting their historical worth or lack thereof. Over time a coterie of students, and not necessarily the history stars, began to make our office their Friday afternoon hangout. At first they sat on the floor and listened. In due course, one brave soul decided to give his opinion about a movie we were discussing; his example emboldened the others. After one of

---

[3] Jacques Barzun, *Begin Here: The Forgotten Conditions of Teaching and Learning*, (Chicago: The University of Chicago Press, 1991), 199.

these Friday sessions, a student came to talk to me. He had had an epiphany. As he described it, "All of you (the history department) really love this stuff. It's not just a job for you. You live it. So teaching history is who you are." The student had witnessed several well-made selves in action, grounds from which trust germinates.

But what's the carry over, if any, between a school like Alden and those most American children attend? At first glance it seems nothing at all. Isn't it obvious, some would argue, that Alden's excellence is a consequence of a self-selection process that creates a homogenous student body of the gifted and the wealthy? How can schools that charge tuitions most families can't afford and instruct students who enjoy privileges most of their peers don't, serve as models for schools that provide instruction for diverse student populations funded by local taxes? It's like comparing apples to oranges.

That line of reasoning is a cop-out its supporters use to appear as if they are troubled by the lack of educational equity. In fact, they are unwilling to mobilize the political will to achieve it. Instead their relentless tinkering with half-hearted educational reforms condones a distribution of resources that makes it impossible for a majority of schools to institute policies like those in place at Alden. Yes, there will always be a few outliers who find their purpose under the worst of circumstances. But educational equity means that all should have educational opportunities equivalent to those of the most advantaged.

Without the requisite material resources, a school can't begin to foster the perception of its students as persons capable of and responsible for discovering their purposes. Instead that recognition becomes a privilege reserved for the few who can either afford private schooling or who are lucky enough to live in districts with generous school budgets. There's a price to pay for casting this recognition as an elite entitlement. It spawns the inequality that corrupts democracy. It increases the probability that students from less privileged backgrounds will live their lives without having had a full opportunity to discover their possibilities and capacities. Without that self-awareness, a person will find it impossible to imagine how she might achieve excellence, let alone marshal the discipline to pursue it.

What would be gained if there were the political will to make what works at Alden available to all? We have a dysfunctional meritocracy, which legitimates in the fortuitously advantaged a sense of entitlement, a conceit that they have earned what they have been given. Instead we need to recover our original intent of equal educational excellence for all. Doing so would provide the public with an infusion of talent and capabilities from as broad and varied a swath of the population as possible. It's an old ideal. In fact, for Thomas Jefferson it would amount to taking the first step towards realizing his dream for the American republic—to create an aristocracy of everyone.